HEROI

THE EARL

By the Rev. Dr. Newton.

SCENE IN ANCIENT ROME

Christians thrown to the lions in the Amphitheatre."

Page 24.

HEROES OF
THE EARLY CHURCH

BY THE

Rev. Richard Newton, D.D.

Author of " The Reformation and its Heroes,"
" Rambles Through Bible Lands,"
" The King's Highway,"
&c. &c.

SOLID GROUND CHRISTIAN BOOKS
BIRMINGHAM, ALABAMA USA

Solid Ground Christian Books
2090 Columbiana Rd, Suite 2000
Birmingham, AL 35216
205-443-0311
sgcb@charter.net
http://solid-ground-books.com

Heroes of the Early Church
Life-Changing Lessons for the Young

Richard Newton (1813-1887)

Solid Ground Classic Reprints

First printing of new edition July 2005

Taken from 1889 by Thomas Nelson and Sons, London

Cover work by Borgo Design, Tuscaloosa, AL
Contact them at nelbrown@comcast.net

*Cover image is a likeness of Polycarp Before the Proconsul.
This incident is recorded on page 33 of this volume.*

ISBN: 1-59925-000-4

Prefatory Note.

THESE graphic sketches of the " Heroes of the Early Church" are the latest series penned by the distinguished author, whom Spurgeon fittingly called "The Prince of Children's Preachers." The sketches are in many respects the best work of the gifted man. As he ripened in saintship for heaven, his literary style became even more rich with the aroma of the gospel, and so more forcible, simple, and crisp, than in his earlier writings.

The articles were originally prepared for *The Youth's World*, and were issued in that periodical. The revision and preparation of them for publication in this form has been an easy and delightful task. Indeed, so carefully did Dr. Newton prepare his copy for the press that little was required to be done beyond the omission of some repetitions of statement, necessarily incident to serial articles in a periodical. Dr. Newton had planned another series on the "Heroes of the Modern Church," to follow these, but was compelled by ill-health to give up writing them. Yet he continued to work so diligently that the last article from his pen was written for the number of *The Youth's World* which appeared the month after his death. He was conscious that the "Master's call" might come suddenly to him. In view of this sudden "translation," he committed to me the work of revising and issuing these sketches in a permanent form. With great regret he gave up the continuance of the series he had intended, as this note shows :—

"Chestnut Hill, Philadelphia,
"Rev. E. W. Rice, D.D.   *April 9, 1887.*

" My dear Brother,—I return the enclosed papers to you, and am very sorry to be obliged to say that it will not be in my power to go on with the new course of articles on ' The Heroes of the Modern Church'......I am greatly interested in this work, and should like nothing better than to go on with it if I could.   But this is impossible."

A week later came another letter :—

" Your kind letter of yesterday is received.   I never did anything in my life more reluctantly than to write the letter sent you the other day about discontinuing the articles on ' The Heroes of the Modern Church.'   I have always considered it one of my highest privileges to be connected with the American Sunday School Union, in the noble work it is doing for the glory of God and for the good of men.

" And nothing but a sense of *absolute necessity* would ever have induced me to take this step."

Two weeks later there came another letter, showing the sweet submission and strong hope of the Christian in the deepest sorrow :—

                                         " *April 30, 1887.*

" My dear Brother Rice,—I have been passing through deep waters for the last few weeks, in the loss of my dear wife, after we had journeyed on together in the pilgrimage of life for half a century.   All life's other trials seemed light in comparison with this ; and yet I never felt the power and preciousness of the gospel as I have done in going through this trial."

Then came a final note, in his own hand, written from his bed of sickness, from whence he soon after passed to the better land.

Chestnut Hill - Philad[a]
Tuesday Noon

My Dear Brother Rice

Many thanks for yr last last kind letter, & its contents, wh came to hand some days ago. I shd have acknowledged it before, but, for what I am sure you will be sorry to hear; viz - that in the middle of last week, I had a dead break down, fr a severe attack of heart trouble, resulting fr the heavy mental sorrowful strain thro' wh I have been passing for weeks. I am laid on my back & am unable to do anything. I can only wait the Lord's will, as to what the issue shall be.

Yr loving friend & brother

Rich[d] Newton

A few days later on—May 25, 1887, in his seventy-fifth year—Dr. Newton departed to be with Christ.

The gifted author has sketched the characters of these " Heroes of the Early Church" with a loving, vigorous, and graphic pen, which will give young Christian readers of to-day a vivid impression of the greatness and goodness of the men who laboured and sacrificed their lives in the early extension and strengthening of our common evangelical faith.

EDWIN W. RICE.

PHILADELPHIA, *Sept. 1, 1888.*

Contents.

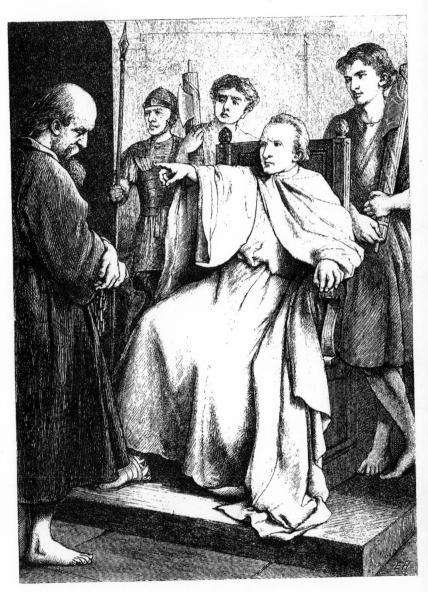

POLYCARP BEFORE THE PROCONSUL.

"Eighty and six years," said Polycarp. "I have served my blessed
Saviour. How can I forsake him now?"

Page 33.

HEROES OF THE EARLY CHURCH.

I.

Clement of Rome.

BORN A.D. 30 (?); DIED A.D. 100 (?).

WE now propose to study the history and
character of some of the Heroes in the
earliest ages of the Christian Church. We will begin
with the first century of the Christian era. The good
man whose name stands at the head of this chapter
was the friend and companion of the great apostles
Peter and Paul. Origen says he is mentioned by
Paul in his epistle to the Philippians. In the fourth
chapter and the third verse of this epistle the apostle
is sending a message to some member of that church,
and he beseeches him to " help those women which
laboured with me in the gospel, with Clement also,
and *with* other my fellow labourers, whose names *are*
in the book of life." Here, perhaps, we have the

good man whose story we are now sketching brought before us.

As we study the principal facts in his life he comes before us as an example of four important practical lessons.

1. Clement of Rome was *an example of earnestness in seeking for the truth*. He was born in the first century of the Christian era. Of course, in his early education he was only taught about the gods whom the heathen worshipped. But this teaching did not satisfy him. The great question which troubled him was, " Will my soul live after the death of my body?" He wished to know if there was any authority for believing in the immortality of the soul. He made up his mind never to rest till this question was settled. But his heathen teachers could give him no satisfaction upon this subject. After hearing all they had to say, he studied diligently the teachings of the Roman and Egyptian philosophers; but they had nothing to tell that gave him any help in settling this important question. Still he determined not to give the matter up.

Then he heard that the Son of God had come down from heaven to give light on these great subjects. This encouraged him to go on with his inquiries, in the hope that he should at last find out the truth about this matter.

Soon after this, tradition says that he became acquainted with the apostle Barnabas at Rome. He followed him to Alexandria, and then to Judæa. At Jerusalem, Barnabas introduced him to the apostle Peter. Peter gave him all the information he had so long been seeking for, about the soul and its salvation. The true doctrine of eternal life was made clear to him. Thus he was brought to the Saviour, and was baptized and joined the church.

2. Clement of Rome comes before us as *an example of humility.* And here let me say that in handling these far-off histories, it is often very difficult to get the actual facts. Outside the Bible there is no authentic history of this early age of the Church. It is only the voice of tradition that speaks to us on the part of Clement's career now before us. What this voice says is that when the apostle Peter knew that his days were drawing to an end, and that the time of his departure was at hand, he was very anxious to have a suitable person selected to take his place as the head of the church at Rome. His intimate acquaintance with Clement satisfied him that he was better adapted for that position than any one else he knew. So he called a council of the church, and urged Clement on their attention as the best person to occupy the important office of bishop of their church.

The term *bishop* is used in these sketches in the New Testament sense, where the word *episcopos* or overseer is applied, and not as implying all that in these modern days is connected with the term bishop.

3. We have in Clement of Rome *an example of*

activity in doing good. He did good by promoting peace. When the Christian church was first established at Rome, it was a divided church. There was one branch known as the Jewish church, and another as the Gentile church; but under the influence of the peace-loving spirit of this good bishop, the prejudices then existing were softened down, and the two parties became one.

Clement had been intimately connected with the church at Corinth. After he was made bishop he heard that there was a very bitter strife in that church, growing out of the parties into which it had been divided. This distressed him very much; and here his love of peace came into play again. In the hope of allaying that bitter strife, and bringing the opposing parties there together in unity, he wrote his famous epistle to the Corinthian church. This epistle was written in such an humble, gentle, loving spirit that it subdued the bitterness of the strife existing there, and acted on the disturbed church of Corinth very much as oil acts when poured on the surface of the troubled waters.

This epistle in its language and spirit is so very much like the epistle to the Hebrews, that the members of the early Church regarded it as almost equal to the inspired writings, and for the first three centuries of the Christian era it used to be read in the churches, very much as the Scriptures were. Then it was lost to the Church for many centuries, but was discovered again between two hundred and three hundred years ago. Let us all follow the example of Clement as a lover of peace.

Again, he did good by trying to spread abroad the gospel, as well as by making peace. Tradition tells us that he sent ministers to preach the gospel in distant regions, where the glad tidings of salvation had never been heard; and the amount of good which he accomplished in this way will never be known till the great day of final judgment.

4. We have in this hero of the early Church *an example of indomitable courage.* There are no *historical facts* on which we can draw to illustrate this part of our subject. It is only a late tradition that speaks to us here. But the story thus given affords a good illustration of the courage of this good man. And what tradition has to say here is that Clement was always trying to use his personal influence in such a way as to bring those about him who were not Christians to a knowledge of Jesus as their Saviour. In this way he was the means of the conversion of a noble lady named Theodora; and also of her husband, who was a kinsman of the emperor Nerva, and a great favourite with him. This led the emperor to begin a very severe and cruel persecution. Clement of Rome did not escape this persecution. He was seized and cast into prison. When the time of his trial came, he had to make his choice between sacrificing to the idols of Rome and being sent into

banishment. And here the courage of this brave man was well shown : he refused to sacrifice to the idols. Then the sentence of banishment was issued against him. He was sent away from Rome to a far-off place called Cherson. This was a little town beyond the Pontic Sea. On arriving there, he found those banished like himself were compelled to labour in the mines. They had to endure the severest labour and the most terrible hardships. They were whipped and beaten and chained ; their heads were half shaved, their right eyes bored out, their left legs disabled, and disgraceful marks were branded on their foreheads ; and in addition to all this, they were exposed to hunger and thirst, and cold and nakedness. Clement found great numbers of Christians there condemned to all these miseries with himself. They were delighted to have so noble a Christian as he was to be their companion in suffering. Then he began to hold services and to preach the gospel to them after their day's work was done. Many of the heathen people from the surrounding country attended these services. Great numbers of them were converted. Before long the heathen temples in that region were deserted.

When the emperor heard of this, he sent an officer to stop this Christian work by persecution. But, finding that putting the common people to death did not stop the work from going on, he resolved to make an example of one of the leading men among them ; so Clement was chosen for this purpose. He had to make his choice between renouncing his religion and being put to death. Here again he displayed the same courage which had animated him before. He refused to give up his religion. Then he was condemned to death. He was put on board a small vessel and carried far off from the shore. A heavy stone (or, according to another account, an anchor) was fastened to his feet, and he was plunged into the depths of the sea. Such, tradition says, was the end of this hero of the early Church.

But when we think of Clement of Rome, let us remember the four good lessons taught us by his example—the lesson of earnestness in seeking for the truth, the lesson of humility, the lesson of usefulness, and the lesson of courage—and let us try to imitate his example in these respects; and then God's blessing will rest upon us, and we shall be successful in our life-work.

II.

Ignatius of Antioch.

BORN A.D. 30 (?); DIED A.D. 107 TO 117 (?).

W E come now to consider Ignatius, the second in our list of Heroes of the early Church.

About the exact time and place of the birth of Ignatius, and his parentage, we have no certain knowledge, and therefore on these points we shall not attempt to say anything. Only this remark may be made: that if the statement is correct which represents him to have been about eighty years of age when he died, and if that event took place in the year 116 or 117, then he must have been born between the years 30 and 40 of the Christian era.

Ignatius always used to speak of himself as Ignatius *Theophorus*. This is a Greek word which means being borne or carried by God. And every one who is trying to be a true Christian may well be thus spoken of. For we are clearly taught in the Bible that God's everlasting arms are under all his followers, and his sheltering wings are over them.

It has been reported that Ignatius was the very

child that our Saviour took up in his arms when he wished to teach his disciples the great lesson that they must be converted and become as little children if they wished to be his true followers. It would be an interesting circumstance in the history of this good man if we could know that this was a fact; but this cannot be known, and so we merely refer to the circumstance and pass it by.

Ignatius in his earlier years had the privilege of receiving instruction from the apostles Peter and Paul. He not only heard them preach in public, but was also favoured with their more familiar teachings in private. While thus intimate with the apostles just mentioned, he tells us himself that he was the disciple of the apostle John. Under the instruction of these great and good men, he was taught "the truth as it is in Jesus;" and then, in view of the thorough knowledge he had of the gospel, as well as of his great piety and the excellent gifts which God had bestowed upon him, he was chosen by the apostles to be the head and ruler of the church in the city of Antioch. This is a city which has had a very interesting and important history. It was founded about three hundred years before Christ, and is situated on the river Orontes, sixteen miles from the Mediterranean Sea. It stands on a beautiful plain surrounded by ranges of mountains. The temples and palaces of Antioch were of the very finest kind. A wide avenue ran through the centre of the city, about four miles long, on either side of

which was a covered way supported by marble
columns. Antioch was one of the most famous cities
of the East. The rulers and great men of Syria made
it their head-quarters. It was at the height of its
prosperity in the days of Ignatius, and we are told
that it then had a population of four hundred thousand inhabitants. One of the things of greatest interest to us in the history of this city is that the disciples of our blessed Lord "were first called Christians
at Antioch."

It has been nearly destroyed a number of times by
earthquakes, and is now only a small city, with a
population of not over ten thousand.

But this famous city was the scene of the labours
of Ignatius for about forty years; and in studying
the history of this good man's life, we find illustrations of four lessons which it is very important for us
all to learn.

1. *The lesson of practical wisdom.* To know just
what to do and how to do it, is the grand secret of
success in all our life-work. This secret Ignatius
possessed. The times in which he lived were times
of persecution, trial, and difficulty. His position, at
the head of the church at Antioch, was like that of a
pilot steering his vessel through a dangerous channel,
where rocks on one hand and shoals on the other are
constantly presenting the danger of shipwreck. When
false teachers were engaged in efforts to spread abroad
erroneous doctrines, he sought in every way to guard

his people against these dangers by simple, earnest, and untiring statements of the truth as God had revealed it in his Word. Thus the members of his church were preserved from the dangers to which they were exposed, and were helped to cling faithfully to the truths of the gospel in spite of the errors that were then prevailing. And when the days of persecution came upon the church, he was untiring in his efforts to strengthen those who were weak, to encourage those who were depressed, to point them all to that almighty arm on which they were permitted to lean, and to tell them of that omnipotent grace which would be sufficient for them in every time of need, and would bring them off at last more than conquerors through Him who had loved them and given Himself for them.

And when we think how successful this hero of the early Church was in finding out just what he ought to do amidst the perplexities that attended his path, and in securing the help and guidance which enabled him for so many years to do all that his important and responsible position made it his duty to do, we may learn a useful lesson for ourselves; for the same wisdom which guided him to see what he ought to do, and the same grace which enabled him to do it, are just what we need, and just what God will give us if we seek them from him, as Ignatius did.

2. The life of this good man teaches us *the lesson of patient endurance*. Trajan, the Roman emperor,

visited Antioch early in the second century of the Christian era. He had just gained a great victory over the Scythians and the Dacians, and was preparing for a war with the Parthians and the Armenians. He entered the city with great pomp and parade. One of his armies had been defeated by the Christians in another part of his empire. This made him very angry. He began to persecute the Christians in different places; and while staying in Antioch, he made special inquiries about what the Christians there were doing. Ignatius thought it best to call on the emperor and converse with him on this subject. They talked freely about the different religions of the world. Ignatius was honest and faithful in what he said. He told the emperor what the Christian religion was and where it came from. He said there was but one true God, and that is the God whom the Christians worship. He declared that the Christian religion would surely in the end overturn all other religions, and fill the whole world. This made the emperor very angry. He resolved at once to persecute the Christians in Antioch and all through Syria. He began this persecution by ordering Ignatius to be cast into prison. This was done at once, and the good man was subjected to the most severe and unmerciful treatment. He was whipped with scourges which had leaden bullets at the end of them. He was forced to hold fire in his naked hands, while the sides of his body were burnt with paper dipped in oil. His feet were placed on burning coals, while the flesh was torn off from his limbs with red-hot pincers.

But he bore all this without a murmur. His tormentors looked on with astonishment at his perfect endurance. They could not understand it. But when the emperor saw that no amount of torture could make any impression on this heroic man, he pronounced the sentence of death upon him, and ordered that he should be bound in chains; and appointed a company of ten soldiers to conduct him to Rome, where he was to be thrown as a prey to the wild beasts.

And now some of our readers may be ready to ask, " Well, how did Ignatius bear all this ? Did his patient endurance continue ? " It did ; for when he heard of the cruel decree which the emperor had pronounced against him, these were the words he uttered : " I thank thee, O Lord, that thou hast been pleased thus perfectly to honour me with thy love, and hast thought me worthy, with thy holy apostle Paul, to be bound with iron chains." Then we are told that he cheerfully embraced his chains ; and having prayed earnestly for his church, and commended it with tears to the Divine care and protection, he delivered himself into the hands of the soldiers appointed to transport him to the place of execution.

Surely Ignatius was a hero ! How wonderful the grace of God was that could enable him to exercise such patient endurance! Let us all seek that grace, and it will enable us to endure with the same patience any trials that we may have to meet.

3. The third lesson we find illustrated in the history of Ignatius is *the lesson of untiring diligence.* It is a long journey from Antioch to Rome even in our days, but it was much longer in the days of which we are speaking. The question has often been asked why Ignatius should have been sent so far just to be put to death. Many reasons have been suggested for it. The most probable motive for it may have been that the sight of such a well-known person being carried in chains to Rome to be devoured by wild beasts, for the single reason that he was a Christian, might make the people in the countries through which he passed unwilling to think of becoming Christians, lest they might meet with such an end.

The journey of Ignatius from Antioch to Rome was attended with many incidents which helped to make it interesting. In the different towns where he stopped, the ministry and members of the churches there and from the country around would meet together to see and talk with this aged servant of Christ who was going to meet a martyr's death. They would have religious exercises together; they would ask his prayers and his blessing, and he would ask them to remember his much-loved church at Antioch in their prayers. Ignatius was an aged man at this time; and when we think of the many years of hard labour which had occupied him, we should hardly have expected that, while pursuing such a long journey and bound in chains, he would still keep busily at work. Yet this was what he did. When they stopped on their journey, he was busy writing all the time. He wrote to his friends at home, the members of the church for which he had laboured so long and so faithfully. Then he wrote to the churches in the regions of country through which he passed, exhorting them to be faithful to their Christian calling, and entreating them to pray for his church at Antioch. Some six or more of these epistles have come down to us. This is the way in which Polycarp, a dear friend of Ignatius, who lived at the same time, speaks of these epistles: "They contain," says he, "instructions and exhortations to faith and patience, and whatever is necessary to build us up in the religion of our Lord and Saviour Jesus Christ."

And when we think of this hero of the early Church working in this way while on his last journey to meet a martyr's death, we may well speak of him as illustrating beautifully for us the lesson of untiring diligence. And this is a lesson which we should all try to learn and practise.

4. The closing scenes of the life of this good man illustrate *the triumph of faith.* When he was approaching Rome, the Christians of that city came out to meet him. They met him, naturally enough, with

mingled feelings of joy and sorrow. They were delighted to have the presence and company of so great and good a man; but this pleasure was greatly marred when they thought how soon and by how painful a death he was to be taken from them.

The authorities of Rome concluded that his martyrdom should take place on one of their great festivals, so that his punishment might be more public. Accordingly, on the 29th of December, in the year 116 or 117, he was brought out into the amphitheatre, and the lions were let loose upon him. They were not long in doing their work, but quickly devoured him, and left nothing but his bones. These the friends who came with him on his journey gathered up and carried back to Antioch.

And thus, as a martyr, Ignatius gave the highest testimony to his fidelity to the truth of that religion which he had preached and practised. He gloried in his sufferings. When he looked upon the chains that bound him, he called them his jewels and ornaments; and he laid down his life with as much ease and comfort as another man would put off his clothes. And though the death he had to undergo was cruel and barbarous, yet the thought of it had no more effect upon his mind than the dashing of the ocean's waves upon the solid rock. These were the last words that he spoke, before he was led out to the lions: " Let the fire, and the cross, and the assaults of the wild beasts, and the breaking of bones, come upon me, so that I may be with Jesus my blessed Saviour. I would rather die for Christ than live and reign the sole monarch of the whole world!"

Surely in the death of this hero of the early Church we have a splendid illustration of the triumph of faith.

III.

Polycarp of Smyrna.

Born a.d. 60 to 80 (?); Died a.d. 167 to 169 (?).

WE come now to study the history of the third of our heroes of the early Church; and in considering it our attention may be given to two leading points: these are *the facts of Polycarp's life*, and *the truths illustrated in them*.

The place of Polycarp's birth is nowhere definitely stated. It is generally supposed, however, that he was born at Smyrna, which was the scene of his life's labours. The time of his birth is not distinctly stated either. At the time of his martyrdom, which is said to have taken place about the year 167 of the Christian era, he declared that he had been serving Christ for eighty-six years. This doubtless referred not to the years of his natural life, but to his Christian life, or to the years in which he had been working for his Saviour. And if we suppose that he was fifteen to twenty years old when he became a Christian and joined the church, then he must have been over a hundred years old at the time of his death; and according to this, he must have been born between the years 60 and 70 in the first century of the Christian era. Early in life he became a disciple of the apostle John, and was taught the truths of the gospel by him and other apostles who had seen and conversed with our blessed Lord in the flesh.

By the apostle John he was put in charge of the church at Smyrna; and he spent the years of his long life in earnest and successful labours for its welfare.

Smyrna, the scene of Polycarp's ministry, is a famous city in Asia Minor. It lies at the head of a gulf of the same name. It is an ancient city, founded by Theseus in B.C. 1312, who named it after his wife. It has a population of one hundred and thirty thousand. It is situated on a beautiful plain surrounded by mountains. Its domes and minarets and tall cypress trees give it a splendid appearance. It is generally supposed to be the birthplace of Homer, the famous Greek poet. Here Polycarp lived and laboured all the days of his life; and here, when the persecution broke out under the Emperor Marcus Antoninus, he ended his course by a martyr's death, being burned at the stake, it is said, in the year 167 of the Christian era.

Such are the leading facts in the history of this noble hero of the early Church.

And now let us look at some of the lessons which we find illustrated in this history.

There are four of these of which we wish to speak.

1. We have in Polycarp's life *a good illustration
of the way in which God's providence takes care of
his people.* Polycarp was born in poverty. When
he was a mere child, he was sold to some one for a
trifling sum. Now if you or I had seen this poor,
ignorant child when he was sold into slavery, how
little we should ever have expected to hear of him as
becoming a great and useful man in the world! Yet
so it was. But how was this unexpected result
brought about? By the wonderful working of God's
providence. There was a noble Christian woman
then living in Smyrna whose name was Callisto.
She had a dream one night in which an angel appeared to her. The tradition is, that the angel told
her about this child Polycarp, and directed her, in the
name of God, to send for the child, to redeem him
from slavery, and then take him into her own house
and have him educated. She did so; and in that
good Christian home Polycarp was brought up and
received his education. There he was taught about
Jesus and his mission into our world; there he became acquainted with the apostle John. Through
John's influence he was brought into the church, and
was prepared for his great life-work as the head or
bishop of the church at Smyrna.

We could not wish for a better illustration of the
way in which God's providence works in taking care
of his people, and in preparing them for what he has
for them to do, than Polycarp's life affords. And it

would be easy enough to find illustrations of the same kind on every hand. The lives of such men as William Carey, or John Newton, or John Williams, " the martyr-missionary of Erromanga," and of other Christian labourers, would furnish illustrations of just the same kind.

2. We have in the history of Polycarp *a good illustration of earnestness in learning the truth and of diligence in teaching it to others.* The two points now before us—earnestness in seeking the truth and diligence in teaching it—are matters of the greatest importance to us all. In the case of Polycarp, the first of these points is well brought out by a pupil of his named Irenæus. He is one of the heroes who will soon come before us. In writing to a friend of his about Polycarp, he says : " I remember seeing you when yet a boy with Polycarp in Asia Minor. I could even now point out the place where he used to sit and talk to us. I could describe his going out and his coming in, his manner of life, his personal appearance ; and how he used to tell us of his intercourse with the apostle John and with others who had seen the Lord, and the pleasure with which he used to repeat all that he had heard them say about Jesus, about his miracles and his teachings. Polycarp told it all to us as one who had received it from the lips of those who had seen the blessed Lord with their own eyes." Here we see the earnestness with which Polycarp listened to the words of those who

could tell him about Jesus and the truths which he taught.

God says to each of us by Solomon (Prov. ii. 3–6), " If thou criest after knowledge, and liftest up thy voice for understanding ; if thou seekest her as silver, and searchest for her as for hid treasures ; then shalt thou understand the fear of the Lord, and find the knowledge of God." This was just what Polycarp did. He sought the knowledge of God in the way here pointed out, and he found it according to the promise here given. And if we follow his example, we shall be rewarded as he was.

And then, when Polycarp had gained the knowledge of the truth in the earnest way here spoken of, he was diligent in teaching it to others. One way in which he did this was by the faithful preaching which he kept up through all the years of his long life. Another way in which he did it was by the earnestness with which he opposed the prevailing errors of that day. As our Saviour opposed the temptations of Satan in the wilderness by simply saying, " It is written," and then quoting God's written word, so did Polycarp in his contests with the heretics of his day.

And then he showed the same diligence in teaching the truth in his writings, which have come down to us. His epistle to the Philippians is genuine, and the most important of his writings. In speaking of this epistle, one of the early writers calls it " a most perfect epistle." Another writer says, " It is an admirable epistle. From it those who are anxious about their salvation may learn about the gospel of Jesus and the truth which it teaches." It is full of short and useful precepts and rules of life, all of which are sustained and urged by quotations from different portions of the Word of God. This epistle was so highly prized by the early Christians that they used to have it read in their churches just as they did the canonical Scriptures. Thus we see how diligent Polycarp was in teaching the truth which he had been so earnest to learn. And this is what we should all try to do.

3. We have in the life of this good man *an illustration of the honour which God puts upon his faithful servants.* God says to his people, " Them that honour me I will honour." Polycarp honoured God by the readiness with which he received his truth and the faithfulness with which he obeyed his commands. And God honoured him in a very peculiar way by the message which he sent to him from heaven.

In the opening chapter of the book of the Revelation, the seven churches then existing in Asia Minor are mentioned. The apostle John was directed by God to write a letter or epistle to the head of each of those seven churches. The second of those churches was that of Smyrna. This epistle begins thus : " Unto the angel of the church in Smyrna write ; These things saith the first and the last, which was dead, and is alive ; I know thy works, and tribulation, and poverty (but thou art rich)......Fear none of those things which thou shalt suffer......be thou faithful unto death, and I will give thee a crown of life." Now think what an honour it was for God to call Polycarp "the angel of the church in Smyrna." To be called the king or the emperor of the mightiest kingdom in the world would be nothing in comparison with this. The king would soon be obliged to put off his crown and lay aside his sceptre, and let his kingdom pass into the hands of another ; but the Church of Christ, of which Polycarp was one of the angels, is an everlasting Church. And Polycarp's connection with it will be everlasting too. No change will come over that Church, or over those who are the angels, the ministers, or the servants of it, but that which is involved in their everlasting march from glory to glory. And then think of the honour of receiving such a promise as God here gave to Polycarp. It was the promise of "a crown of life," if he proved faithful unto death. In all the world there is no honour to be compared to the "crown of life" here referred to. Let us all try to be "faithful unto death," as Polycarp was, and then we shall share the honour which God gave him.

4. The closing scene in the life of Polycarp *illustrates very strikingly the sustaining power of the grace of God.* Under the reign of the Emperor Marcus Antoninus a very severe persecution broke out

against the Christians. As the most prominent man in the church, Polycarp was seized and put in prison. On the breaking out of the persecution his friends advised him to leave Smyrna, and try to save his life by retiring to a small country town. He did so, but the servants of the emperor followed him there. They found out the house in which he was staying, and called there late at night. He had gone to bed before they came; but when he understood who the men were and what they had come for, he rose and dressed himself. Then he went downstairs and received them as kindly and pleasantly as though they had come to save his life instead of to destroy it. Then he had a supper prepared for them, and insisted on their partaking of it, which they did with the greatest surprise and wonder. After this he gave himself up into their hands, and they took him back to Smyrna and delivered him to the officers of the government. Now, how wonderful the power of God's grace must be which could lead a man to act in this way toward those who were seeking his destruction !

The proconsul, or chief officer of the government, then tried very hard to persuade Polycarp to renounce Christianity and swear by the gods of Rome. Polycarp listened attentively to all he had to say, and then gave this as his noble answer: "Eighty and six years I have served my blessed Saviour. He has done nothing but bless me all the time; then how can I forsake him now?" Then he was led forth to execution. The officers had determined that he should be burned to death. When they reached the place the soldiers were about to nail him to the stake. He begged them not to do that, assuring them that his God, who gave strength to endure the fire, would enable him to stand there without being nailed. Then they only tied him to the stake. And as he stood there, patiently waiting for the fire to be kindled, the words of his prayer were the last he ever spoke: "O Lord God Almighty, the Father of thy well-beloved Son, Jesus Christ, by whom we received the knowledge of thee, the God of angels and of all creatures! I bless thee that thou hast graciously brought me to this day and hour, that I may receive a portion among the number of thy martyrs and drink of Christ's cup. Wherefore I praise thee for all thy mercies; I bless thee and glorify thee through thy beloved Son, Jesus Christ, through whom to thee and the Holy Ghost be glory both now and for ever. Amen." Then the fire was kindled and the flames rose; but instead of wrapping themselves about him, tradition says that they formed an arch of fire over him and left his body untouched. Then the officer in charge ordered one of the soldiers to thrust him through with his spear, which he did. After his body was burned, his Christian friends gathered up his bones and buried them in a tomb, over which a little chapel has been built, on the south-eastern side of the city. That spot has ever been regarded as sacred to the memory of this hero of the early Church.

And when we think of the calm, triumphant way in which Polycarp was able to meet his painful death, we have a splendid illustration of the sustaining power of the grace of God.

IV.

Justin Martyr.

BORN A.D. 105 (?); DIED A.D. 165 (?).

JUSTIN the Martyr is among the earliest of those good men coming before us for our study. The exact year of his birth is not certainly known, but it was somewhere towards the close of the first century of the Christian era. The date of his death is said to have been in the year 165. He was born in the city of Shechem in Palestine. At one time this city was called Neapolis. It is now known as Nabulus or Nablus; but in the time of Justin, it was known as Shechem. It is one of the most ancient cities of Palestine. When Abraham first came into this land, he pitched his tent and built an altar to God under an oak in Shechem. After the ten tribes separated from the kingdom of Judah, Shechem was for some time the capital of the kingdom of Israel. The tomb of Joseph is near this city, and so is Jacob's well, where our Saviour met the woman of Samaria and had that interesting conversation with her, of which we read in the fourth chapter of John's Gospel.

Shechem is one of the most interesting towns of the Holy Land, in its situation. It lies in a beautiful valley between the celebrated mountains of Gerizim and Ebal. When Joshua brought the tribes of Israel into Canaan, he assembled them in this valley, and from the top of Mount Gerizim he read, in the hearing of the people, all the blessings which God had promised should attend them if they obeyed his voice. And then from the top of Mount Ebal he read the fearful curses which were to come upon them if they were not obedient to the commands of God.

When going through the Holy Land we spent two days at Shechem, being detained there by a heavy rain. On the second day, when the rain had ceased, we went up to the top of Mount Gerizim. The prospect was most charming; and while standing there I tried to picture to myself what a sight it must have been when all the tribes of Israel were assembled in the valley below to hear the blessings pronounced upon them from one of these mountains, and the curses from the other.

With this interesting town in Palestine the name of Justin Martyr is intimately connected. He was a man possessed of unusual talents as a writer and a speaker; and although he did not enter the ministry, he was yet one of the most useful men among those of whom we are now speaking, in helping to build up and defend the cause of Christ in the world. And in studying the leading facts of his history, we find in him an example worthy of our imitation in four respects.

1. He is so when we see *what an earnest seeker after the truth he was.*

The father of Justin was not a Christian, and so in his early years he was not taught anything about Christ and his religion. But he had a very inquiring mind, and he resolved, when he was quite young, to find out the truth.

There were then four different schools of philosophy known among men. These were the Stoics, the Peripatetics, the Pythagoreans, and the Platonists. Justin determined to find out the teachings of these different schools and see which was the most satisfactory. He began with the Stoics. This school was founded by Zeno in the third century before Christ. They taught that there were gods, but that they took no interest in the affairs of men; and that these affairs were all ruled by a fate which nothing could resist. Justin soon gave up this school. He next examined the teachings of the Peripatetics. This school was founded by the famous Aristotle in the fourth century before Christ. The meaning of the name is *walkers;* and they were so called because Aristotle always used to walk about when he was teaching his pupils. They taught a great deal about the dignity of human nature, and that all real happiness was only to be found in the proper use of our moral and mental faculties. This did not satisfy Justin, and then he

went to the Pythagoreans. This school was established by Pythagoras, a Greek philosopher, in the
sixth century before Christ. They taught the doctrine
of the transmigration of souls, or, that after death the
souls of men go into the bodies of animals and then
into vegetables and minerals. This did not satisfy
Justin, and so he turned to the Platonists. This was
a school founded by Plato, a Greek philosopher, in the
fifth century before Christ. The teachings of this
school came nearer to the Christian religion than any
of the others. Plato had probably got some of his
ideas from what the Jews in Egypt had told him
about the Old Testament. Justin found the teachings
of this school more satisfactory than those of any of
the others, and as he knew nothing about Christ and
the truth which he taught, he became a Platonist.
He had gone as far as he could go, and proved himself
an earnest seeker after the truth.

2. We see in Justin Martyr *a successful finder
of the truth.*

When we go as far as we can in seeking for the
truth, and yet have not succeeded, we may be sure
that God will help us, and then we shall succeed.
This is just what God teaches us when he says, "Ye
shall seek me, and find *me*, when ye shall search for
me with all your heart" (Jer. xxix. 13).

After Justin became a Platonist, he made up his
mind to retire from the busy world, and choosing a
place by the seaside, he gave himself up to quiet

meditation, and to find out more of that truth which he had sought so earnestly.

One day, as he was walking up and down the sea-shore, rapt in earnest thought, he was met by a grave-looking, venerable man, who asked him some questions about the important subject which was occupying his mind. They were soon engaged in earnest conversation together. Justin told the stranger that he was a believer in the philosophy of Plato. He then stated some of the leading doctrines of that system, and went on to defend them. The meek old man, who was a Christian, listened attentively to all he had to say. Then he told him that the great truth for which he was seeking never could be found in the way in which he was then seeking it. "The schools of philosophy of which you have spoken," said the old man, "know nothing about this truth. And what they have not found themselves, they never can give to others. The pearl of great price does not lie within their range. The thing for you to do, if you wish to find this pearl, is to 'search the Scriptures.' Study the Hebrew prophets. They were taught by the Spirit of God. They saw and revealed the truth on which our salvation depends. Pray God to guide you into the knowledge of that truth. He will hear your prayer and answer it, and in his light you will see light."

This was the turning-point in Justin Martyr's history. He followed that strange old man's advice.

He went home and procured a copy of the Scriptures. Giving up the teaching of Plato, he studied carefully what the prophets of God had written. He prayed to God for guidance. His prayer was heard. The light of truth shone in upon the darkness of his mind. He was led to repentance and faith in Christ. He turned his back on the teachings of the philosophers, and found that it was only "the truth as it is in Jesus" which met all the wants and satisfied all the longings of his soul. And thus the earnest seeker of the truth became the successful finder of it. And what was true then is true now, for God's promise is, "I will be found of them that seek me." Earnest seeking and successful finding of saving truth always go together.

3. We have in the history of this good man *the example of a faithful follower of the truth.*

Justin was a man with intellectual abilities of an unusual character. He had stood very high among the followers of the Platonic school of philosophers, and was one of their most influential members. They were very much troubled to think of losing from their ranks one who had been so eminently useful, and were quite at a loss to understand what could have led him to make such a change. Then he wrote a long letter to them, explaining the reasons which had led to his conversion. In commencing this letter he uses these words:—

"Think not, O ye Greeks, that I have rashly and

without deliberate judgment departed from the rites of your religion. I was obliged to make this change, because I could find nothing in the teaching of your philosophy which could meet the longings of my soul, and give me that rest and peace of mind without which I never could be happy. Your wisest teachers never can give satisfactory answers to the questions of those who are anxious to find rest and peace for their souls."

Then he went on to show the folly of all that their philosophy taught. And he wound up his letter in such words as these :—

" Come now, O ye Greeks, and listen to the voice of heavenly wisdom ; be instructed in a divine religion, and acquaint yourselves with a King who is immortal. Become as I am, for I was once as you are. These are the reasons which led to my conversion. The doctrine of the Christian religion is divine and satisfactory. It subdues the corruption of our fallen nature, and gives us the victory over our evil passions ; and when these are subdued, the soul experiences a joy and happiness which can be found nowhere else. It is reconciled to its Creator, and finds all it can need in him."

This was the way in which Justin Martyr followed out the truth which he had found in the religion of the gospel. And though he was not a minister, and preaching was not his life-work, yet we can readily understand how much good he must have done to all

about him by speaking and writing of the gospel of
Jesus in such a way as this. God said to Abraham,
" I will bless thee, and *thou shalt be a blessing.*" And
what God said to him, he says to you and to me, and
to all who are successful finders and faithful followers
of the truth, as Justin was. By the words we speak,
by the prayers we offer, by the works we do, and by
the example we set, we may be blessings to all about
us, as this hero of the early Church was.

4. We find in this good man *the example of a
brave defender of the truth which he had sought and
found and followed.*

He was not satisfied with explaining the gospel to
his friends, but was always ready to stand up in its
defence against all its enemies wherever he met with
them. In one of his visits to Rome he encountered a
prominent Jewish teacher named Tryphon, who was a
great enemy of Christianity, and went about teaching
that Jesus of Galilee was a deceiver, and his religion
a cheat. Justin had a two days' debate with him in
the presence of a large assembly of people; and the
end of it was, that Tryphon confessed that he had
been entirely mistaken about the Christian religion,
and that Justin had taught him to understand the
Old Testament prophets better than he had ever done
before.

And then Justin defended the truth in another
way. Antoninus was the Emperor of Rome at that
time. He was a mild and excellent prince, and did

not persecute the Christians himself; but their enemies falsely charged them with crimes which they had never committed, and so, in different parts of the empire, they were persecuted and put to death under the edicts of former emperors which had never been repealed.

Justin resolved to try to stop this; so he wrote a defence of Christianity, or, as it is called, an apology for it, and sent it to the emperor. This had such a good effect upon him that he published a decree forbidding that the Christians should be persecuted anywhere, unless it could be proved that they were teaching or doing something against the welfare of the Roman Empire.

Some years after this, when Antoninus was dead, and his son Marcus Aurelius had succeeded him as emperor, the Christians were again persecuted. Then Justin wrote another apology for Christianity, and sent it to the emperor. But this was not so successful as his former effort had been. It made the emperor angry. He issued a decree for persecuting the Christians and putting them to death. Then Justin and six of his companions were taken prisoners and brought before the prefect of the city of Rome. He called on them to sacrifice to the gods of Rome. This they refused to do. Then they were sentenced to be scourged and beheaded. This was done.

And thus we see in Justin Martyr an example of an earnest seeker after the truth, a successful finder of it, a faithful follower, and a brave defender of it. Let us ask God to give us grace to follow his example, and then it will be our privilege to be heroes of the Church in this nineteenth century, as Justin Martyr was in the second century.

V

Irenæus of Lyons.

BORN A.D. 120 TO 140 (?); DIED A.D. 202 (?).

IRENÆUS of Lyons is the next hero that comes before us for our consideration. The facts of his history that have come down to us are few. There are various points connected with his life on which it would be interesting to dwell, if we could only obtain further information. But this cannot be had, and so we must make the best of such knowledge as we have. We find this difficulty at the very beginning of our subject. How natural it is to pause just here and ask the question, When and where was Irenæus born? It is easy enough to ask these questions, but it is not so easy to answer them. Indeed, positive answers to them cannot be given.

It is believed that he was born between the years 120 and 140 of the Christian era. And the place of his birth is just as uncertain as the time of it. It is generally supposed that he was born in the city of Smyrna, in Asia Minor, or somewhere in that neighbourhood. There he became acquainted with the good Polycarp, whose history and character we have already considered. From him he received the instruction that he needed to mould his character and fit him for the life of eminent usefulness which he spent in the cause of Christ.

Irenæus was sent by Polycarp to Lyons in France to do missionary work there, and that became the scene of his life's labours.

Lyons is the second city of France for its size and its importance. It is an ancient city, having been founded in the first century before Christ. It is beautifully situated on the rivers Rhône and Saône. Its present population is between three hundred thousand and four hundred thousand. On a hill behind the town, about five hundred feet high, stands a famous church, which is visited every year by a million and a half of pilgrims.

Lyons is especially famous for the silk goods which are manufactured there. Seventy thousand looms are occupied in carrying on this work, and these give employment to 140,000 weavers. The silk goods manufactured in Lyons are sent to almost every part of the world. And for the purchase of the raw materials for those goods, for the wages of the workmen employed thereon, and for the sale of the goods when finished, not less than £40,000,000 are expended every year.

This famous city was the scene of the great life-work of the hero of the early Church whose history is now before us. And in dwelling on this history, Irenæus comes before us as an example worthy of our imitation in three different views that we may take of him.

1. *He is a good example for us to follow when we consider him as a true missionary.*

It was his friend and teacher Polycarp, the head or bishop of the church of Smyrna, who sent him to France. Smyrna was then the great centre of communication with all the eastern part of the world; and Lyons was, no doubt, a place of considerable business importance even then. And its business must have brought it into connection with the leading people of Smyrna in that early day. Thus Polycarp would learn about the state of things in Lyons and in Gaul or France, the country of which it was so important a city. It is supposed that some of the merchants of Lyons, while trading in Smyrna, may have heard Polycarp preach, and, being converted by his preaching, may have begged him to send some one to preach the gospel to the people of their country. And this was probably the reason why he sent Irenæus to them. Irenæus was then a minister of the gospel. He had been thoroughly educated, was a man of fine ability, and an eloquent preacher. There he laboured for years as a devoted missionary. The church of Lyons grew and prospered under his influence. Pothinus, a venerable and devoted man of God, was the head or bishop of that church. In connection with

him, Irenæus spent all his time and strength and
energy in trying to make the gospel known, and to
build up the church in Lyons and through all that
part of France.

After Irenæus had been thus at work for some
years, a fierce persecution against the Christians in
France broke out, under the Emperor Antoninus.
Great numbers of all ranks were put to death. Pothinus, the venerable head of the church at Lyons, in
his ninetieth year, was seized and tortured. Then he
was thrown into prison, and it was arranged to have
him put to death the next day. But before the morning dawned he died in prison. Irenæus was chosen
to take his place as the head of the church in Lyons.

And thus he carried out his mission. It involved
great sacrifice and self-denial on his part, for there
was little or nothing of the education and refinement
in France then that he had been accustomed to among
his own people. But he took up the work appointed
for him in the spirit of a true missionary, and he devoted his life to that work in the exercise of the same
spirit. And the result of his faithful labour was seen
in the growth and prosperity of the church in Lyons
and all the surrounding country. When we think
of this, we cannot wonder to find him spoken of by
those who knew him best as " *the light of the Western
Church.*"

And this is just the spirit which we should all have
and exercise. Our blessed Saviour expects us to be,

as the apostle Paul expressed it, "workers together with him." There is missionary work for us all to do, wherever we may be placed ; and our happiness here and our reward hereafter will depend very much on the faithfulness with which we carry out this missionary spirit.

2. We find Irenæus setting us *a good example for our imitation, when we consider him as a real peacemaker.*

There are two incidents in his history which illustrate this peace-loving element of his character. One of these we see in the efforts which he made to counteract the errors of the sect called the Montanists. These men professed to have received the Spirit of God in a miraculous way, and that they had visions and dreams by which they were led and taught without any regard to the Word of God. The result of their teachings was that the Scriptures were set aside, and men were led into all sorts of erroneous doctrines and practices.

Eleutherus, who was the bishop or pope of Rome at that time, had fallen under the influence of this sect, and was about to give his public sanction to the support of their erroneous views. This was likely to break up the harmony and unity of the Church, and lead to the bitterest strife and contention. The Christians in Lyons, and the martyrs who were then in prison awaiting their death in defence of the gospel, were greatly distressed by this state of things. They wrote earnest letters to the bishop of the church of Rome, begging that the influence of that church should not be used in support of this false teaching, and pointing out the endless strife and contention which would thus be brought upon the whole Church. Irenæus was sent to carry these letters to Rome. For the sake of the peace of the Church he was willing to undertake that long journey. His efforts and influence there were successful. The errors of the Montanists were not endorsed as the teaching of the Christian Church, and this had much to do with preserving the peace and purity of the Church.

The Church of Rome in these days claims to be infallible in its teachings; but certainly it was not infallible when its head, the pope, was ready to hold and teach the erroneous doctrines of the sect of the Montanists.

Some years after this there was another occasion when the Church was in danger of strife and division, but when the influence of Irenæus was again exerted to preserve its peace. This was when the controversy arose about the proper time for keeping Easter. Victor, who was then at the head of the church of Rome, had made up his mind that all who did not hold the same views which he held on this subject should be excommunicated or cut off from connection with the Church. This course, if persisted in, would have led to bitter and endless conflict. A council was called of the principal churches of France to consider this matter. After a careful examination of it, they recommended Irenæus to write a letter to Victor, earnestly remonstrating against the ground he had taken, and entreating him, for the sake of the prosperity and peace of the Church, to change his course and to allow the members of the Church everywhere to hold their own opinions about keeping Easter, as there was no authoritative teaching on the subject in the Scriptures, and it was not a matter on which any one's salvation depended. Here his efforts were again successful, and thus he proved himself to be a true peacemaker. And this is what we should all try to be. Jesus our Saviour came to bring " peace on earth." He is the " Prince of peace ;" his gospel is the gospel of peace ; and all his people should strive so to live and act that the precious promise may be theirs which says, " Blessed are the peacemakers : for they shall be called the children of God."

3. Irenæus comes before us as *the example of an earnest worker.*

We might find in his history various illustrations of this point of our subject, but the work he did with his pen is that of which we desire especially to speak.

Many different sects, teaching erroneous doctrines, sprang up in connection with the Church in the latter part of the second century. These sects led many persons away from the simple truth as taught in the Scriptures. This was a great cause of grief and sorrow to the honest-hearted, truth-loving Christians.

But no one felt this more than Irenæus did, and he resolved to do all in his power to correct this evil.

The chief of these erroneous sects was called the Gnostics. They took this name from the Greek word signifying knowledge, because they claimed that they knew more than any other people about what was really worth knowing. But they were mistaken in this. Not satisfied with the simple teachings of the Bible, they went off into all sorts of wild speculations about the origin of evil, the eternity of matter, and similar subjects. These discussions led them into endless errors. Irenæus made up his mind to see what he could do to counteract these errors, and he spent six or seven years of his life in seeking to accomplish this object. He gave himself up to the careful study of the teachings of these different sects; and then, in the light both of reason and of Scripture, he tried to show the errors contained in them, and the sad results to which those errors must lead. He wrote a number of volumes on this subject. Various titles were given to them, but the short, simple name by which they are best known is, "Against the Heretics." Only a portion of what he wrote has come down to us; but enough of his writings remain to fill two large octavo volumes of between four hundred and five hundred pages each. A very nice edition of this work was published in Edinburgh a few years ago. It is called "Irenæus against Heresies." When I took up one of these volumes and examined it, I could not help having a feeling of awe and reverence for it. I said to myself, " Here is a work that was written seventeen hundred years ago. How many minds have been influenced by it! How many wanderers in the paths of error have been brought back again to the simple truth of God through the teaching of these books! What an untold amount of good must have been done by these writings of Irenæus! And how glorious the harvest he will reap in heaven from the seed sown in the earnest work which he did for God in connection with the church at Lyons!"

Irenæus lived till the early part of the third century. He died some time between the years 202 and 208. Whether he died a natural death or ended his course by martyrdom is not certainly known. But he was a real hero of the early Church; and it will do us good if we try to follow his example when we think of him as a true missionary, a real peacemaker, and an earnest worker.

VI.

Clement of Alexandria.

BORN A.D. 160 (?); DIED A.D. 220 (?).

CLEMENT, of whom we are to speak next in our list of famous men, is said to have been born in the year 160 of the Christian era, and to have died in the year 220. He is sometimes spoken of as an Athenian and sometimes as an Alexandrian. The explanation of this is that Athens was the place of his birth, and Alexandria the place where his principal life-work was carried on. Thus his name is naturally connected with two of the most famous cities of the world. We may say a few words about these cities before going on to consider the history of Clement.

Athens, the place of Clement's birth, is the principal city of Greece. It is said to have been founded by Cecrops, fifteen hundred years before Christ This was about the time when Moses was keeping the flock of Jethro, his father-in-law, in the land of Midian. What a far-off period that seems to be! It would require a large volume to give the history of Athens in detail. The city is beautifully situated around the base of the celebrated hill called the Acropolis. This hill is about three hundred feet above the city, and six hundred feet above the level of the sea. Athens is distant between four and five miles from the sea, and used to be connected with the well-known harbour of the Piræus by a wide avenue, protected on either side by a high solid wall. There is probably no other city in the world which has been connected with so many famous men in every department of life, as warriors, philosophers, historians, musicians, poets, artists, and in all the pursuits that have occupied the thoughts and called forth the energies of man, as has Athens. The statues and temples of Athens have had no equals in the world. The most famous of these is the temple called the Parthenon. It was built by Pericles more than four hundred years before Christ, and was considered the finest temple in the world. The ruins of the Parthenon are still standing, and no one who enjoys the privilege of looking at them will ever forget that sight. There used to be in this temple a gigantic statue of the female divinity Athena, after whom this city is named. It was nearly fifty feet high, was all made of gold and ivory, and cost about £100,000. But the most interesting thing about this city to Christians is the fact that here Paul, the great apostle of the Gentiles, stood on the top of Mars' Hill and preached Christ to the philosophers and wise men of Athens. In this famous city Clement, the subject of our present study, was born.

And as he was connected with Athens by his birth, so he was connected with Alexandria by the great work of his life. This was another famous Eastern city. It was founded by Alexander the Great, and named in honour of himself, between three hundred and four hundred years before Christ. It is situated on the south-eastern shore of the Mediterranean Sea, and near the mouth of the Nile. It used to be the great centre of trade and commerce between the eastern and western portions of the world. This made it very prosperous. At one time its population amounted to six hundred thousand, though now it does not exceed two hundred thousand. It was for centuries the royal abode of the rulers of Egypt. In this city was said to have been collected the largest library the world had then known. When the Turks took possession of this city, in the early part of the seventh century, the caliph Omar is said to have ordered this library to be destroyed. His reason for giving this order was thus expressed : " If these books contain only what we find in the Koran, they are not needed. If they teach anything different from what the Koran teaches, then they are injurious, and had better be destroyed."

Two famous obelisks used to be seen outside the limits of this city, near the Nile. They were called " Cleopatra's Needles," and were objects of great interest to travellers. I remember the pleasure with which I gazed upon them when there some years ago. But those obelisks are no longer to be seen there. One of them was presented to England, and has been set up on the bank of the river Thames. The other was presented to our country, and now stands in Central Park, New York.

But now for Clement. We have not so many incidents connected with his life as we have had in connection with the other heroes we have considered. But from the little that we do know of him we may learn three good practical lessons.

1. The first lesson taught us by the life of this good man is about *how to find the truth.* He was an early and an earnest seeker of the truth. He was born in a heathen family, and had no home influences about him to lead him in the right way. He was blessed with excellent natural abilities ; and as soon as he was old enough to act for himself he determined to begin at once, and never rest till he had found out what the truth is about God, about the soul and eternity.

Athens, the city of his birth, was always famous for its learning. The different sects of philosophy had their schools there. Clement applied to them, and listened attentively to all they had to teach. But this did not satisfy him. Then he resolved to leave home and seek elsewhere for further light. He visited all the places in the Eastern world which were most celebrated for their learning, inquiring eagerly for the truth. It was a long and trying experience through which he passed. He gained a little in one place and a little in another; but he never arrived at any clear and satisfactory understanding of what the truth is, till he returned to Egypt and took up his abode in the city of Alexandria. Here he found that there was a large and prosperous school, taught by a Christian minister whose name was Pantænus. Clement joined this school, and listened attentively to all the teacher had to say. There the gospel of Jesus, in its simplicity and fulness, was made known to him. This met his wants and satisfied his longings. It was to him like cold water to a thirsty soul. Clement was an early and an earnest seeker of the truth, and he found it. And those who thus seek it will be sure to find it. There are two of God's precious promises which make this certain. In one of these God says, " Those that seek me early shall find me " (Prov. viii. 17). In another he says, " Ye shall seek me, and find *me*, when ye shall search for me with all your heart " (Jer. xxix. 13). To seek and find the truth in Jesus is the most important thing for us all to do. We never can be happy, we never can be truly useful, till we know this truth. And so the first and most important thing for us all to do is to seek this truth, and never to rest till we find it. Let me entreat all my readers to follow the example set by Clement of Alexandria, and be early and earnest seekers for the truth.

2. The second lesson we may learn from this good

man is *how to use the truth for our own good when
we have found it.*   When the way to heaven was
pointed out to Clement, he did not say, " Now I know
the way.   That is enough.   I can walk in it at any
time."   No ; but when he understood what that way
was, he began to walk in it at once.   When he learned
that Jesus was the Great Physician, whose " balm of
Gilead " was the only medicine to cure sin-sick souls,
he did not put off the taking of that medicine till
some future time.   No ; but he took it at once, and
was made whole by it.   When he made up his mind
to be a Christian, he did not trouble himself to find
out what other Christians thought and felt, and said
and did.   He took the Word of God as " the man of
his counsel " and his guide, and resolved to follow its
teachings in all things.   Like the apostle Paul, his
prayer in reference to every point of duty was, " Lord,
what wilt thou have me to do ? "   The knowledge of
the truth which Clement had gained made him a consistent Christian ; and this is what it will do for us
if we make a right use of it.   Just see how useful
consistent Christians may be.

When Lord Peterborough lodged for several days
with Fénélon, the archbishop of Cambray, he was so
delighted with his humble, earnest piety, that he said
on leaving, " If I stay here any longer, I shall become
a Christian in spite of myself."

A young minister, when about to be ordained, said
to a friend, " At one time in my life I was very near

becoming an infidel; but there was one argument in favour of Christianity which I never could get over, and that was the beautiful and consistent example of my father."

Clement of Alexandria had never seen the sweet lines which Charles Wesley wrote to show how the knowledge of the truth he had gained led him to consecrate his life to God's service, but he acted in the very spirit of those lines. Wesley says:—

> " Lord, in the strength of grace,
>   With a glad heart and free,
> Myself, my residue of days,
>   I consecrate to thee.
>
> " Thy ransomed servant, I
>   Restore to thee thine own;
> And from this moment live or die
>   To serve my God alone."

Let us all do this, and then, like Clement, we shall be using the truth for our own good.

3. In the third place, Clement used the truth, when he had found it, for *the good of others as well as for his own good.* One way in which he did this was by his example. When he had found out what the truth in Jesus was, he carried out its teachings faithfully in his daily life. And there is no telling the amount of good we may do to others in this way. Here is an illustration. We may call it one act of a boy, and what good it did.

Some time ago a little boy went home from a ragged school in London, with his dirty face washed clean. When his mother saw him she hardly knew him, but she liked the change. It pleased her so much that she washed her face. When her husband returned from his daily work, he was so surprised at the change which he saw in his wife and son that he went to work and washed away the grime and dust from his hard and dirty hands. So it spread through the family. Then the neighbours saw and admired the change, and very soon that dark and dismal alley, so long the abode of dirt and filth, became noted for its cleanliness. And all this resulted from one good act of that little boy.

Again, Clement's use of the truth enabled him to do good *by his teaching* as well as by his own example. When Pantænus, the teacher of the famous school at Alexandria, died, Clement was ordained to the ministry, and appointed in his place as the head of that school. He occupied this position for all the remaining years of his life. Here he had a large number of pupils under his instruction; and those pupils, when they had finished their studies, went out to occupy positions of great influence and usefulness in different parts of the Church. And all the good accomplished by those good men may be traced to the teaching of Clement.

And then by *his pen*, or by what *he wrote*, as well as by what he did and said, Clement made use of the truth for the good of others. He wrote a number of volumes, but only three of them have come down to us. The first of these is called " Exhortations to the Gentiles." His aim in this work was to point out the errors taught by the different systems of religion in the heathen world, and then to show in contrast with them what the teachings of the Scriptures were. This was useful in bringing many souls to Christ. The second of his works was called " The Pedagogue," or " The Instructor." In this work he brings out the character of Christ as the Great Teacher, and shows clearly the principles which he appoints for regulating the thoughts and feelings, the words and actions of his people. This was especially intended to be a help and guide to those who had renounced heathenism and become Christians. They found this work very useful to them in trying to become earnest and consistent followers of Jesus. The third and last work of this good man had for its name the Greek word " Stromata," which means, literally, *a collection of pieces.* It was made up of selections from different portions of Scripture, which he had found profitable to himself, and which, by adding plain, practical remarks to them, he tried to make useful to others. And so, when we think of the earnest efforts which Clement made to find the truth, and how, when found, he used it for his own good and for the good of others, he comes before us as an example which we shall all find it useful and profitable to follow.

VII.

Tertullian of Carthage.

Born a.d. 150 to 160 (?) ; Died a.d. 220 to 240 (?).

TERTULLIAN, who is the subject of our present chapter, was a friend of Origen.

In the life of this distinguished man we have brought before us the most ancient of the Latin fathers of the Church. His works, many of which have come down to us, have won for him a position of great prominence in the early Church. He was born about a.d. 160, and died in his seventieth year, about the year 230. The place of his birth was the celebrated city of Carthage.

This city is said to have been founded by the famous queen Dido, of whom Virgil, the Roman poet, has so much to say in his work called the "Æneid." The origin of Carthage dates back as far as the ninth century before Christ. Its first inhabitants came chiefly from the city of Tyre, in Phœnicia. It was situated on a bay of the Mediterranean Sea, not far from the present city of Tunis. Carthage was founded many years before Rome, and in its earlier history was a flourishing and important city. It is said to have had at one period a population of seven hundred thousand inhabitants. For a long time it was the great rival of the city of Rome. The Carthaginians and the Romans were engaged in frequent wars together. The chief contests between them were those so well known in history as the first, second, and third Punic wars. In carrying on those wars Scipio was the most famous of the Roman generals, and Hannibal of the Carthaginians. The Romans finally conquered the Carthaginians, and destroyed their celebrated city in the year 140 B.C. It remained in ruins for more than a hundred years. In the first century of the Christian era, the emperor Augustus rebuilt the city and gave it its old name, and it had a flourishing history again for several hundred years; but it was finally destroyed by the Saracens about the middle of the seventh century, and now nothing remains of its ancient grandeur except a few broken arches, the ruins of a great aqueduct that was fifty miles in length. What an illustration the history of this once famous city affords us of the vanity of earthly greatness!

In that famous city, Tertullian, the subject of our present study, was born. His father was a Roman centurion in the service of the proconsul of Africa. The natural abilities of Tertullian were very great. He was educated for the civil service of the empire, and was specially designed by his father to be a Roman lawyer. We know comparatively little of the details of Tertullian's life ; but from what we do know of his history, we can draw illustrations of three important lessons.

1. Tertullian comes before us as *an example of deci- sion.* He was over thirty years of age when he first be- came acquainted with the Christian religion. He had entered fully into the business for which his father had trained him, which was the practice of a Roman lawyer. He was getting on very successfully with that business, and had the prospect of attaining great distinction in his profession. Just then he was brought to a knowledge of the truth as it is in Jesus, and felt disposed to become a Christian. But if he took this stand, and professed himself a follower of Christ, he knew very well that it would be a dis- advantage to him in his business prospects, and would occasion him great pecuniary loss. The question for him to settle was, " Shall I continue to worship the gods of my fathers, or shall I give them up and take Jesus as my God and Saviour ? " This was a very important question for him to decide. He was then just in the position which Paul occupied when Jesus appeared to him on his way to Damascus to persecute the Christians. Paul had been brought up at the feet of Gamaliel, the most famous Jewish teacher of that day. He had the prospect of great success before him as a Jewish lawyer ; but he knew very well that if he became a Christian it would ruin all his prospects of worldly success. And yet he made up his mind to take this course. He saw and felt that the loss of

all earthly things would be a gain, if he could only win Christ and become a partaker of the untold blessings which were to be found in him. And Tertullian had just the same experience here. Like Paul, the great apostle, he began his Christian life with a noble act of decision. And this is the way in which every Christian life should be begun and continued. We cannot be true Christians in any other way ; and the practice of such decision always does good to ourselves and enables us to do good to others. How many examples of this we have !

When Alexander was asked how he had conquered the world, his answer was, " By being decided."

Here is an example of the effect of decision. A little girl was awakened at a meeting where the story of the leper whom Jesus healed was read and talked about. The leper came to Jesus and worshipped him, saying, " Lord, if thou wilt, thou canst make me clean. And Jesus put forth *his* hand, and touched him, saying, I will ; be thou clean. And immediately his leprosy departed from him." In speaking about this afterwards to a friend, that little girl said, " When I got home after the meeting I went to my own room to think about what I had heard. I said to myself, ' I noticed that there was an *if* in what that man said to Jesus ; but there was no *if* in what Jesus said to him.' Then I knelt down and said, ' Lord Jesus, thou canst, thou wilt make me clean. Now I give myself to thee.' " That little girl's decision made her a

Christian at once. This brought great good to her, and made her the means of doing great good to others.

2. We have in Tertullian *an example of consistency,* as well as of decision. Not long after he became a Christian, he had occasion to visit the city of Rome and to spend some time there. During his stay in Rome he was very much grieved to find how differently most of the professing Christians there lived from the way in which he lived himself, and in which he felt sure that all true Christians should live. They engaged in worldly amusements, and practised selfish indulgences of various kinds, very much as people were accustomed to do who did not profess to be Christians. This was something which Tertullian could not understand. He felt sure that Jesus expected his people to " come out from the world, and be separate." He felt sure that John was right when he said, " If any man love the world, the love of the Father is not in him." For himself, he was satisfied that he did love the Father, and therefore that he could not and ought not to love the world too. He made up his mind that if he was to be a Christian at all, he would be a true, honest, and faithful Christian ; that he would have " the same mind which was in Christ," and would " tread in the blessed steps of his most holy life." But when he saw the mass of professing Christians about him living so differently, he was at a loss to know what to do.

While in this state of perplexity he became ac-

quainted with some members of a sect in the Christian
Church called the Montanists, after the name of their
founder, Montanus.   He made careful inquiries about
the principles and practices of this sect.   He found
that they held all the fundamental doctrines of the
Scriptures, only that they claimed to have the gift of
prophecy still in exercise among them.   But the thing
which chiefly interested Tertullian in this sect was the
faithfulness of their practice as Christians.   They gave
up all worldly pleasures and amusements, and faithfully carried out the Scripture principle of self-denial
in reference to everything which the Scriptures taught
them to be contrary to the will of God.   This agreed
entirely with his own views of what Christians ought
to do and be, and so he joined this sect.   He felt sure
that he could not be a consistent Christian without
acting in regard to worldly things just as the members
of that sect acted; and in doing this he was only
carrying out the principles of true consistency.   When
a person desires to become a member of the Episcopal
Church, one of the questions asked is this: " Dost
thou renounce the devil and all his works, the pomps
and vanities of this wicked world, and all the sinful
lusts of the flesh, so that thou wilt not follow nor be
led by them ? "   And the person usually answers: " I
renounce them all, and by God's help will endeavour
not to follow nor be led by them."   Though Tertullian
did not use these words, yet he made his profession
in the very spirit which these words set forth, and he

carried out that spirit through all the course of his Christian life; and in doing this he was only setting an example of true consistency. And if all the members of the Church of Christ would make some such vow as we have just referred to, and would carry it out as consistently as Tertullian did, what a blessing it would be to the Church and to the world! Consistency is an honour to the cause of Christ.

Alexander the Great had a soldier in his army who bore his name, but was a great coward. Provoked at the inconsistency between the man's name and his conduct, the emperor said to him one day, " Either change your name or act consistently with it." And this may be said to every Christian.

We may close this part of our subject with the following lines of Charles Wesley :—

> " That wisdom, Lord, on us bestow,
>   From every evil to depart,
> To stop the mouth of every foe ;
>   While upright both in life and heart,
> The proofs of godly fear we give
> In showing how true Christians live."

3. We have in Tertullian *an example of usefulness.* He was ordained to the ministry when about forty years of age, and in the faithful discharge of the duties of that high office he proved eminently useful both with his voice and with his pen. In the exercise of his ministry he was not confined to any particular charge, but, like the apostle Paul, he went everywhere,

preaching the glorious gospel. And like Paul he had but one unchanging theme, which was "Jesus Christ, and him crucified." He was a very eloquent preacher, and wherever he went multitudes listened delightedly to the words of life which fell from his lips. We have no particular report of the direct results of his preaching; but in the judgment of the great day, when the results of human actions are made manifest, in the number of souls brought to Christ by his preaching we will see how useful he was with his voice.

But then with his pen he was even more useful than with his voice. Truth *spoken* soon dies away, and its usefulness ceases; but truth *written* remains a living power for generations. The writings of Tertullian were not so numerous as those of Origen, whose history we will soon consider, but they were of the same character. He wrote controversial works. These were designed to meet and counteract the various forms of error which prevailed in those days. Then he wrote many practical works to explain and enforce different parts of Christian duty. He wrote on repentance, on faith, on baptism, on prayer, on patience, on the resurrection, on Christian faithfulness, and on many other subjects; and if we could only follow out the influence of his writings on different members of the Christian Church, not only in that age but in the ages which followed, we should be able to form a correct idea of the extent of the usefulness of this good man. And if God shall give us grace to follow the example of Tertullian in the *decision* and in the *consistency* which marked his course, then like him we shall find our lives made useful to all about us.

Sydney Smith used to say, " Try to make at least one person happy every day. Try this for ten years, and then you will have made three thousand six hundred and fifty persons happy." Work like this is worth living for ; and if we are thus useful while we live, our usefulness will continue when we are dead. " Luther is dead ; but the Reformation still lives. Calvin is dead ; but his vindication of God's free sovereign grace will never die. Knox and Melville and Henderson are dead ; but Scotland still retains a Sabbath and a Christian peasantry, a Bible in every home and a school in every parish. Bunyan is dead ; but his bright spirit still walks the earth in his ' Pilgrim's Progress.' Baxter is dead ; but souls are still quickened by his ' Saint's Rest.' Henry Martyn is dead ; but who can count the quickened spirits that have been started into life by his example and his memory ? Robert Raikes is dead ; but the Sabbath schools which he started are living still, and carrying blessings round the world." Let us be as useful as we can while we live, and then our usefulness will continue when we die.

VIII.

Origen of Alexandria.

BORN A.D. 185 (?); DIED A.D. 254 (?).

ORIGEN is the next in the catalogue of these great and good men. He might well stand at the head of the list. There were none among them more gifted with natural abilities, more eloquent as a preacher, more eminent in piety, more diligent in study, more advanced in every branch of learning, and more extensively useful, than he was.

Origen was born in the city of Alexandria, in the year 185 of the Christian era. His father, Leonidas, was a man of learning and a devoted Christian. This faithful father took charge of his son's early education. He instructed him in all the different branches of human learning that were then known, and was particularly careful to make him fully acquainted with the principles of the Christian religion, so that, like another Timothy, from a child he knew the holy Scriptures, which were able to make him wise unto salvation. In these he was well instructed and thoroughly exercised; and he diligently improved the privilege thus granted him. Part of his daily task was to learn and repeat to his father some passage of Scripture. He took great delight in doing this; and often, after reciting those passages of Scripture, would ask his father questions about them which he found it very difficult to answer.

In the year 202, when Origen was seventeen years old, during the persecution that raged under the Emperor Severus, Leonidas was put in prison, tortured, and suffered martyrdom. While his father was in prison, Origen, young as he was, had a great desire to be a martyr, and would gladly have gone with his father to prison and to death. He wrote letters to his father, beseeching him not to change his mind nor give up his faith in Jesus. His mother had great difficulty in keeping him from joining his father in prison, and she actually had to hide his clothes to keep him from going out and exposing himself to danger.

In the early years of his life, Origen was a pupil in the celebrated school at Alexandria, and received there the instruction of Clement, who was then the head of that school, and whose life-work we studied in a previous chapter. On the death of Clement, Origen was appointed to take his place as the head of that school. His life was one of abounding usefulness. He shared in the persecutions which prevailed in those days, and was imprisoned and tortured on several occasions. But he always bore these sufferings as became a real hero, which he was. And at last he died at the city of Tyre in Palestine, in the year 254. And so, as Dr. Philip Schaff has well said, " he belongs among the *confessors,* if not among the *martyrs,*" of the early Church. His tomb, near the high altar of the cathedral of Tyre, was shown for many years, until it was finally destroyed during the wars of the Crusades.

It would require a larger space than we can give to take in all the details of the history of this great man's life ; but we can draw out from it illustrations of four important practical lessons, which it will be well for our readers to remember and to follow.

1. We find in the early life of Origen *an example of filial devotion.*

On the death of his father the government seized and confiscated all the property which belonged to him. This left the mother and six children, of whom Origen was the eldest, in utter poverty and want. What was to be done ? With the charge of such a family on her hands, it was impossible for the mother to earn anything for their support. But young Origen stepped nobly forth for the help and comfort of his mother. He was then only seventeen years old, yet he gave up his position as a pupil in the famous school of Alexandria and opened a school of his own. God smiled upon his efforts and made them successful. Thus he was able to provide for the support of his mother and her family. But Origen never

would have risen to the position of honour and usefulness which he afterwards occupied, if it had not been
for the loving devotion to his mother which he
practised. God's blessing always follows such devotion. Here is a striking illustration of this from
modern history. We may call it *filial affection.*

Gustavus III., the King of Sweden, while passing
on horseback one day through a village near his
capital, observed a peasant girl, of pleasing appearance, drawing water from a fountain by the wayside.
He went up to her and asked for a drink. In a
moment she lifted her pitcher and very respectfully
put it to the lips of the monarch. Having satisfied
his thirst, he kindly thanked his benefactress, and
said,—

" My young friend, if you will go with me to
Stockholm, I can give you a more agreeable occupa-
tion than that you now have."

" Ah, sir," she replied, " I'm much obliged to you,
but I cannot accept your offer. I am quite satisfied
to remain in the position where God has placed me;
but, even if it were not so, I could not on any account
change my present situation."

" Why not ? " asked the king with some surprise.

" Because," said the girl, blushing, " my mother is
poor and sickly, and has no one but me to help and
comfort her in her trials; and no offer which any one
might make could tempt me to leave her or neglect
the duties which affection requires of me."

" Where is your mother ? " asked the king.

" In yonder little cabin," pointing to a wretched-looking hovel near by.

The king, who was very much interested in the girl, went with her into her humble home. There, stretched on a bed of straw, lay an aged female, pressed down with age, sickness, and infirmities. Moved by what he saw, he said to the aged sufferer, " I am very sorry, my friend, to find you in such a sad state."

" Ah, sir," said the poor woman, " I should deserve to be pitied indeed, were it not for that darling daughter. She labours for my support, and leaves nothing undone that she thinks will be a help and comfort to me. May a gracious God remember it to her for good ! " she said as she wiped away her tears.

Gustavus never felt so happy as he did then, to think that he had it in his power to afford help where it was so much needed. He slipped a purse of money into the hand of that faithful daughter, and said, " Continue to take care of your mother. I will soon help you to do it more effectually. Good-bye, my friend."

On his return to Stockholm, he settled a pension for life on that mother, and this, when she died, was to go to her daughter. And God blessed Origen for his filial devotion in much the same way.

2. We find in Origen *a good example of self-denial.* In trying to help his mother, and to show the

reality of his religion, he determined to carry out
faithfully our Saviour's words when he said, " If any
man will be my disciple, let him DENY HIMSELF." He
made it a matter of principle to give up everything
that was not indispensably necessary. He refused to
receive the gifts of his pupils. He had but one coat,
and took no thought for the morrow. He seldom ate
any flesh ; he never drank wine or intoxicating liquor.
He devoted the greater part of the night to prayer
and to the study of the Scriptures, and slept on the
bare floor. And this earnest self-denial on his part
added very much to his influence and to the power of
his teaching. It secured for him the respect and the
confidence both of the learned and the unlearned
among his pupils, in an age and country where such
a mode of life was held in the highest esteem both by
Christians and heathen. This was one of the things
which led his friends to call him Origen the *Adaman-
tine.* The adamant is one of the hardest and most
unchanging of minerals, and they thought he was a
sort of living adamant. And thus, in connection with
his public and private instructions, he was the means
of making many converts from pagans of all ranks.
By the good example of self-denial which he set forth,
Origen was simply making all about him know and
feel that there was a reality in the religion which he
professed. And this is the way in which a good example will always make itself felt. We may do good
by our words, but we can do much greater good by

our actions. Here is an illustration of this point. We may call it *the power of example.*

In the fourth century the emperor Constantine had one of his armies commanded by a brave and noble general. In marching through a distant part of the empire, this army on one occasion was nearly starved for want of food. Approaching a town inhabited by Christians, the general sent one of his officers to ask provisions for his army. The Christian people of that town immediately supplied their wants. Wondering at their free and noble charity, the general inquired what kind of people they were, to be so generous. He was told that they were Christians, and that their religion taught them to hurt no one, but to try to do good to all. This had such an effect on Pæhmius that he never rested till he became a Christian. Then he resigned his position in the army and became a minister in the Church of Christ, and spent the rest of his days in preaching peace instead of making war.

3. We have in the life of this good man *an example of faithfulness to the truth.*

We see this in the great efforts he made to preserve the truth in its purity, and to spread it abroad on every hand. He was known to be such an eloquent preacher, and so successful in his efforts to correct false doctrines and teach those that were true, that bishops and leading men in all parts of the Church, when they found those about them who were teaching false doctrines, would send for Origen to come and correct their errors, and proclaim among their people the simple " truth as it is in Jesus." And he was always ready to answer these calls, and was eminently successful in the efforts thus put forth. He would supply his place in the school of which he had charge, and then would go forth cheerfully wherever he was called, to arrest the progress of error and uphold the cause of truth when it was in danger.

And in thus showing his faithfulness to the truth, Origen was treading in the footsteps of the great apostle Paul. When Paul saw in his night vision a man beckoning to him and saying, " Come over into Macedonia, and help us," he obeyed the call without any regard to the toil or danger to which it might expose him. The principle on which he acted is thus set forth by the apostle : " Neither count I my life dear unto myself, so that I may finish my course with joy, and the ministry which I have received of the Lord Jesus, to testify the gospel of the grace of God." This was the way in which Paul showed his faithfulness to the truth ; and this was what Origen did, and what God expects us all to do.

4. Origen comes before us as *an example of untiring industry in his efforts to spread the truth.*

When he had accomplished the different missions of which we have just spoken, he hastened back to his home at Alexandria, and laboured patiently in the arduous work of his school there. By diligent study he had mastered all the different systems of philosophy which were taught in those days. He drew out from them whatever truths were found there that harmonized with the teaching of the Scriptures, and blended them together. This made his school remarkably popular. Pupils came to it from all parts of the world; and great numbers of them became Christians, and went home to spread the influence of the gospel around them in the circles through which they moved.

But it was in *his writings* more than in anything else that Origen's industry was seen. The works that he wrote were more numerous, more learned, and more useful than those of any other author in the early Church. The number of his works is said by some to have amounted to six thousand. This is no doubt beyond the mark, but it shows us how very numerous his works must have been to be thus spoken of. The most important of them were those which he published on the Scriptures. He spent twenty-eight years of his life in this work. Not only his days but large portions of his nights were thus occupied. He used to have seven secretaries and seven copyists labouring with him continually. He wrote fifty volumes on the Scriptures. These were of three kinds:—The first contained short explanatory notes on difficult passages of Scripture, designed especially for young Christians; the second contained full expositions of whole books of Scripture, for the instruction of more advanced students; and the third was made up of exhortations or practical applications of Scripture, for the benefit of the common people. Then he published many doctrinal works on the subjects of controversy which prevailed in the Church in those days. He also wrote a number of works on the practical duties of religion. There were many different versions of the Scriptures in those days. These varied from one another very much, and good people were often at a loss to know which was the true version, on which they might depend and by which they might be guided. Origen devoted a great deal of his time to this department of study. He examined the Hebrew and Greek and other versions of the Bible with untiring industry, and published the result of his study in such a form that all earnest Christians might know satisfactorily just what the true Word of God was, which they could take as " the man of their counsel and their guide." Very few of these numerous works of Origen have come down to us, but none can tell the amount of good accomplished by them among the members of the early Church.

Now when we think of Origen let us remember the example he has set us of filial devotion, of self-denial, of faithfulness to the truth, and of untiring industry in spreading it. Let us pray for grace to follow his example, and then we shall bear blessings wherever we may go.

IX

Cyprian of Carthage.

BORN A.D. 200 (?) ; DIED A.D. 258 (?).

THE interesting characters we are now considering take us over a large period of the history of the Christian Church—from the time of the apostles nearly to the dawn of the Reformation. In this great field of study we find characters and incidents that have an air of freshness about them, and that prove both instructive and profitable.

Among the heroes of this early period to which we would next call attention is Cyprian, the bishop of Carthage.

This city was, in its day, one of the most famous cities of the world. It was situated in the northern part of Africa, near where the city of Tunis now stands.

Carthage is the city which is said to have been founded about eight hundred and fifty years before Christ, or a hundred years before the foundation of the great city of Rome, as we found when studying about Tertullian in a previous chapter.

There are four good points in the character of Cyprian to which we may refer.

1. We may speak of him as *an example of diligence.*

Cyprian is believed to have been born in the year 201, or the first year of the third century of our era. His family was highly respectable, and his father was one of the senators of the city of Carthage. Of course he was brought up in the heathen religion which prevailed in his country. He was first a student and then a teacher of the laws of Carthage; and he had pursued his studies with such unusual diligence that he was considered the ablest teacher of the law in Carthage.

He remained an idolater till he was over forty years of age, then he became a Christian. And whether we look at him as a private Christian or as a minister or bishop, we find the same diligence marking his life and character. This made him successful in everything he undertook; and it will have the same effect on all of us if we learn and practise the same important lesson of diligence. The words of Solomon were true of Cyprian in the far-off times in which he lived, and they are just as true of us who are living now: "Seest thou a man diligent in his business? he shall stand before kings" (Prov. xxii. 29). This simply means that diligence will lead to success.

2. Cyprian was *an example of decision,* as well as of diligence.

He became acquainted with a good Christian minister named Cæcilius, who told him about Jesus and the truths of his religion. Cyprian soon saw how much better this religion was than that in which he had been brought up. He became satisfied that this was the true religion; and though his family and relatives were all idolaters, and were very much opposed to the change he talked of making, and tried all they could to prevent him from making it, yet he resolved to do so. He was baptized in the forty-sixth year of his age. Before this his name had been Thascius Cyprian, but at his baptism he added to this the name of his good friend who had brought him to Jesus, so that as a Christian he was known as Thascius Cæcilius Cyprian. Afterwards through all his Christian life he pursued the same decided course. His mind was quickly made up on all the important questions of the day. He was as diligent in following out the right course as he was decided in choosing it. And here is a good example for all our young friends to follow. The sailor who wants to make a successful voyage must make up his mind as soon as he gets to sea what course he ought to steer, and then he must keep on steering in the right course till his voyage is ended.

3. We find in Cyprian *an example of liberal piety.*

He lived honestly and freely up to the meaning of our Saviour's words when he said to all his disciples,

"Freely ye have received, freely give." When he became a Christian he was very rich. Among his possessions was a fine large house which he used as his home. It had a beautiful garden connected with it which he enjoyed very much. But he sold that valuable property, and set apart the money received from the sale of it for the relief of the poor. That was very noble in him.

In the course of his ministry, his friends, who were very much attached to him, showed their love to him by buying this property and giving it to him again. But while he was busy in his life-work as bishop of Carthage, a very severe famine prevailed in that part of Africa. Thousands of the inhabitants of Carthage died during that terrible visitation. The sufferings of the sick and poor at that time were dreadful. And then Cyprian showed his liberality by selling that property the second time, and using the money it brought him for the relief of the sick and starving poor. And what a beautiful illustration we have in this singular experience of Cyprian, of the truth of Solomon's words when he says, " He that hath pity upon the poor lendeth unto the Lord; and that which he hath given will he pay him again " (Prov. xix. 17). We may be very sure that when we give anything to the Lord's poor he will pay us back in some way; but in Cyprian's case this promise was literally fulfilled, and the very property which he lent to the Lord by giving to the poor, the Lord gave back to him. Let us remember this lesson of Cyprian's liberal piety, and try to follow his example.

4. We find in Cyprian *a splendid example of courage.*

While he was engaged in his work as bishop, that dreadful disease known as the plague broke out in the city of Carthage. Multitudes of people who could afford to do so left the city while this pestilence was raging; and those who could not get away were afraid to enter the houses in which the disease was known to prevail. There were large portions of the city in which thousands and tens of thousands were sick and dying with no one to nurse or wait upon them. And here the courage of Cyprian shone forth. He not only, as we have seen, spent his money for the relief of the sick, suffering, and neglected ones, but he devoted his time in personal attention to them, and, aided by some of his clergy, went from house to house ministering to their wants. This was courage of the highest character. The worshippers of idols were amazed at it, and many were thus led to become Christians.

And then we have a still more striking example of the courage of Cyprian in the way in which he met his death. Valerian, the Emperor of Rome, had issued a decree which required that all Christians should be put to death who would not give up their religion and sacrifice to the idols of Rome. Galerius Maximus, the proconsul of Carthage, in obedience to this decree, summoned Cyprian to appear before him. When he was brought into his presence Maximus said to him, " Art thou Thascius Cæcilius Cyprian ? "

" I am," was the answer.

" Art thou he," asked Maximus, " who hath borne the highest offices of their religion among the Christians ? "

" Yes," said Cyprian.

" The emperor commands that you offer sacrifice to the gods of Rome," said the proconsul.

" I will not offer sacrifice," replied Cyprian.

" *Be persuaded*," said the proconsul, " *for your own sake.*"

Cyprian's reply was, *"Do as thou art ordered; nothing can move me from the stand I have taken."*

Then the sentence was pronounced : " Let Thascius Cæcilius Cyprian be beheaded ! "

" THANKS BE TO GOD !" said Cyprian.

" Let us die with him !" exclaimed the Christians around him.

Then the brave martyr was led away to an open field outside the city, followed by a crowd of Christian friends. He put off his outer garments, and stood calmly waiting the end, clad in a long white robe. Then he kneeled down and commended his soul to God in earnest prayer. After this he tied the bandage over his eyes with his own hands. Then one of his friends fastened his hands behind his back. He ordered a sum of money in gold, equal to five pounds with us, to be given to the executioner, in order to show that he had no unkind feeling toward him. Then he bowed himself to the earth, and was beheaded with a single stroke of the sword. So ended the earthly life of this good and holy man.

Let us remember his example, from the four different points of view from which we have now looked at it, and let us ask God for grace to follow him in the diligence, the decision, the liberal piety, and the courage which we find illustrated in the life of Cyprian, the martyr bishop of Carthage.

X.

Eusebius of Cæsarea.

Born a.d. 260 to 270 (?) ; Died a.d. 338 (?).

EUSEBIUS was a native of Palestine. He was born about the year 264 of the Christian era, and died about the year 340. The place of his birth is somewhat uncertain, but it is generally believed that he was born at Cæsarea, which was the principal scene of his life's labours. He held the office of bishop or head of the church there for more than a quarter of a century. Of his family and early life we have no knowledge ; but he was a diligent student in his youth, and devoted himself to the thorough examination of both the Christian and the heathen antiquities. And the result of these earnest studies is to be seen in the character which he won for himself. Next to Origen, he was the most learned of the ancient fathers of the Church, and from his writings he has always been spoken of as " the father of ecclesiastical history."

Before going on to speak of some of the lessons which his history furnishes, we may say a few words about Cæsarea, the place of his birth and labours, and also of two very important events which took place during the years of his life.

Cæsarea was a flourishing town in Palestine on the Mediterranean coast. It was situated about half way between Joppa and Carmel, and was built by Herod the Great, who gave it the name it bore in honour of Cæsar, the Roman emperor.

The towns in Palestine on the Mediterranean coast have no natural harbours to protect them from the swell of that vast sea, whose waves break along the shore continually with great violence. To afford protection to vessels that might come to Cæsarea, Herod built a great sea-wall or breakwater in front of the town. This was built in a circular form, so as to make a safe harbour for the vessels that might come to trade there. It swept around from the south and west of the town, with an entrance into it from the north. There was room enough in that harbour for the largest fleets that might have occasion to anchor there. This breakwater was built of immense blocks of stone, brought from a great distance and sunk to the depth of twenty fathoms, or sixty feet, in the sea. Herod was occupied in this work about twelve years, and the amount of money expended upon it was immense. Broad landing-wharves surrounded the harbour. A beautiful temple was built in the town and dedicated to the emperor, and in it there was placed a colossal statue of him. Other splendid buildings were also erected in the town; and when they were finished Herod fixed his abode there, and made it the civil and military capital of Judæa.

Cæsarea was the scene of several interesting circumstances mentioned in the New Testament. The conversion of Cornelius, the first-fruits of the Gentiles, took place here. This was the residence of Philip the evangelist. Here Paul resided for some time on returning from his third missionary journey. Here he was imprisoned for two years, and made his famous speech before Festus and King Agrippa. And it was here also, in the amphitheatre built by his father, that Herod Agrippa was smitten of God and died, as we read in Acts xii. 21–23.

It was in this city that Eusebius was born, and served God as bishop of the church for so many years. But now, all the glory of this place has passed away. The ruins of its former splendour are all that remain of it. Travellers through Palestine seldom think of visiting Cæsarea; and the only tenants of its ruins are snakes and scorpions, lizards, wild boars, and jackals.

And now we will consider two important events which took place during the lifetime of Eusebius. One of these was the change in the government of the Roman empire. During the lifetime of the other heroes of the early Church of whom we have already spoken, all the emperors of Rome were heathen men; and they were all engaged, more or less, in persecuting the Christians in different parts of their empire. And this work of persecution still continued in the early part of the history of Eusebius. But during his lifetime a great change took place, and persecution ceased.

The Roman empire was then divided into two parts, the eastern and the western empire. Constantius was ruling over the western empire and Galerius over the eastern. Constantius died in the year 306, and appointed his son Constantine, afterwards called "the Great," to succeed him. The Roman soldiers proclaimed him emperor, and he took possession of the countries of Gaul, Spain, and Britain, over which his father had reigned. Then he engaged in war with Maxentius, who had usurped the governments of Italy and Africa. Constantine conquered Maxentius in three battles. The last of these was at the Milvian bridge, under the walls of Rome. It was during this campaign that the wonderful event took place, in connection with Constantine, which led to the change in the government of the Roman empire above referred to. Eusebius gives us the account of this strange event. He tells us that while Constantine was engaged in this warfare with Maxentius, he saw a vision in the heavens, in which a flaming cross appeared to him, bearing this inscription in Latin :—

" IN HOC SIGNO VINCES."

Translated into English the meaning of these words is, "By this sign thou shalt conquer." Eusebius also informs us that Christ appeared to the emperor in a dream the following night, and directed him to take for the standard of his army an imitation of the fiery cross which he had seen. Constantine caused a standard to be made in this form, which was called "Labarum." This was carried in advance of all other standards, was looked upon with adoration by the Christian soldiers in the army, and was surrounded by a guard of fifty picked men.

Lactantius, a well-known Christian writer of this period, confirms the above statement about Constantine. He also tells us that from this time the emperor confessed himself a Christian, and gave orders that the sign of the cross, with the name of Christ connected with it, should be put upon the shields of all his soldiers, and that they were thus to go forth against their enemies. After this, in the year 313, Constantine published his memorable edict of toleration in favour of Christianity, and ordered that all the property which had been taken from the Christians during the times of persecution should be restored to them. They were also made eligible to any public offices, which had not been the case before. This striking event marked the triumph of Christianity and the downfall of paganism as the ruling power in the empire of Rome. From this time persecution ceased throughout the empire, and peace and prosperity attended the gospel in its progress.

The other great event which took place during the

lifetime of Eusebius was the holding of the famous Council of Nice. This was the first of the great councils of the Christian Church which have been held from time to time. It took place in the year 325. Nice or Nicæa, where this council was held, was a large and flourishing town in Bithynia of Asia Minor. The council held there was the most important of any of the general councils of the Church. It was called together by the emperor Constantine for the purpose of considering the great doctrine of the divinity of our blessed Saviour, and of stating the views of the Church on that important subject.

A new sect had arisen in the Church, under the leading of a minister whose name was Arius. He taught that Jesus Christ was not a divine being, but only a creature. This, of course, took away the doctrine of the atonement. For, if Christ had not been a partaker of the divine nature, he never could have made an atonement for the sins of the human race. Such teaching led to the most serious controversies in the Church. And we cannot wonder at this; for when the divinity of Christ is denied, the foundation on which all the most precious and important truths of our holy religion rest is taken away. There seemed to be no other way of settling this great matter than by calling a council of the whole Church to consider this subject, and to state clearly what the real truth was in reference to it.

It was this view of the matter which led Constantine to call the council of the Church to meet together in the city of Nice. Three hundred and eighteen bishops were present at this council, representing every portion of the Christian Church. In connection with the divinity of Christ, they had many other of the important doctrines of the Bible to consider. Their sessions were continued for two whole months. And, as a result of their deliberations, they declared the truth as held by them, not only on the subject of the divinity of Christ, but on all the other leading doctrines of the gospel. The statement of truth which they set forth is called " The Nicene Creed." This creed is held and used by the Church of England and the Protestant Episcopal Church in this country to the present day. In reference to our Lord Jesus Christ, this creed declares that he is " the only-begotten Son of God, begotten of the Father before all worlds ; God of God, Light of light, very God of very God, begotten, not made, being of one substance with the Father ; by whom all things were made." No more important statement of truth was ever made by man than that which is embodied in this creed. And we may well thank God that the Council of Nice was led to prepare and publish it for us. And when we think of Eusebius, it is pleasant to connect his name with a work which had so much to do with preserving through all ages " the truth as it is in Jesus."

And now we come to consider the history of Eusebius's own life. In this there are two points of view from which we may think of him, and each of them teaches us an important lesson.

1. From the facts of his history we see him acting as *a faithful and an unfailing friend.* He had a friend named Pamphilus to whom he was very much attached. Pamphilus was a minister of the church at Cæsarea. He was a very learned man and a most earnest and devoted Christian. He wrote a number of useful works, and spent a great part of his time in copying portions of the Bible, and giving them away to those who desired to know the way of salvation.

What we are to tell you happened during the reign of the emperor Maximianus, who was a great persecutor of the Christians. He once came to Cæsarea to celebrate his birthday. This was done with great parade and show. To make the exhibitions more impressive, a number of Christians were brought out to be tortured and put to death. Among these was Pamphilus, the friend of Eusebius.

In the presence of the emperor he was called upon to renounce Christianity and sacrifice to the gods of Rome. He refused to do this, and neither threats nor promises could lead him to change his mind. Then the emperor was very angry, and ordered him to be delivered to the tormentors. They racked his sides and tore off the flesh with red-hot pincers. But he stood as firm as a rock and bore his torture calmly. Finding that no impression could be made upon him, he was sent back to prison and was kept there for two years. And it is just here that the faithfulness of his friend Eusebius comes into view. Not all the disgrace and torture inflicted on Pamphilus could keep Eusebius away from him. He was a constant visitor to him in prison. He soothed his sorrows, alleviated his sufferings, and was constantly striving in every possible way to cheer and comfort him. They read and studied together, and wrote such articles as were called for by the necessities of the times, to comfort those who were suffering from persecution, and to strengthen the faith of all in the teachings of Scripture. And it was because of this strong attachment of Eusebius to his friend, and his unfailing faithfulness to him in the time of trouble, that their names were blended together and he was called Eusebius Pamphili. And the example here set us of faithfulness in friendship is one that we should all try to follow. Many of the friends we meet with in this life are only friends in prosperity : when trouble comes, they turn away and leave us. But it was not so with Eusebius, and it should not be so with us. The old proverb says, " A friend in need is a friend indeed." And the opposite statement is equally true ; for one who is not a friend in need is not a friend indeed.

2. Furthermore, in studying the history of Eusebius we find that he sets us *an example of doing good*. He did good in two opposite ways. One was *by what he gathered*, and the other *by what he scattered*. It was by what he gathered that Eusebius was able to write his ecclesiastical history. This was the great life-work with which his name is particularly connected,

This history consists of ten books. These books tell us about all the chief events which took place during the first three centuries of the Christian Church. No one else had ever written carefully on this subject; and if it were not for what Eusebius has written, we should all be in the dark about what took place during those centuries. In writing this history he had to make a path for himself where there had never been a path made before. And the history which Eusebius wrote was not made up of his own thoughts and fancies, but of the actual facts which took place as the years of those centuries rolled on. And how did he get the knowledge of those facts? It was just the diligent gathering of which we are now speaking. He had to go here and there and everywhere gathering information about the men who had been active in the Church's work, and what their activity had led them to do. This was the material out of which the history of the Church in those centuries was made up. It was a possible thing to gather that material together at the time when Eusebius lived; but if he had not gathered it then, it would have been too late for any to gather it after he had passed away. And so we see how all the good which has been done by the ecclesiastical history which Eusebius wrote is to be traced up to his diligence in gathering. He followed out, literally, our Saviour's command to his disciples, after feeding the hungry thousands with five barley loaves, when he said, " Gather up the fragments that remain, that nothing be lost." Eusebius did good by what he gathered, and we may do the same.

But then Eusebius *did good by what he scattered,* as well as by what he gathered, and we may follow his example here also. A letter has been preserved which was written to Eusebius by the emperor Constantine about the year 330. His name had been recently given to the great city which has ever since been called *Constantinople,* and he had transferred to it the seat of his empire. In the letter referred to, the emperor speaks of his great interest in this city, and his desire for its spiritual improvement. He gave Eusebius authority to have several churches built there at his expense. And he especially expresses the great desire he felt to have the Holy Scriptures circulated through that city. There was no Bible-house in Constantinople then, as there is now, where printed copies of the Scriptures could be had. And so the emperor authorized Eusebius to have copies of the Bible written on sheets of parchment and properly bound, and then to be given to the people. This was to be done at the emperor's expense. And this was one of the principal works that Eusebius was engaged in during the latter years of his life.

Eusebius did good *by what he gathered* and *by what he scattered,* and in both these ways he sets us an example which it would be well for us all to follow.

XI.

Athanasius the Great.

BORN A.D. 296 (?) ; DIED A.D. 373 (?).

H ERE we have the name of one of the noblest
heroes and grandest characters in that period
of the Church's history which we are now considering.

Athanasius was born in the city of Alexandria, in
Egypt, in the year 296 A.D., just at the close of the
third century. His life-work ran through the greater
part of the fourth century. For forty-six years he
was the bishop of Alexandria. This was one of the
most famous cities of the East. It was situated on
the northern coast of Africa, near the mouth of the
river Nile. It was founded in the year 332 B.C. by
that celebrated conqueror Alexander the Great. This
city was three miles long and seven miles broad. The
streets crossed each other at right angles, as is the
case with the city of Philadelphia. In the height of
its prosperity, Alexandria is said to have had a population of six hundred thousand inhabitants. In its
size and grandeur it ranked next to Rome, then the
great capital of the world. In its day it was one of the

chief centres of learning in the world. It has passed through many changes since then, but still continues a flourishing city, with a population of about sixty thousand.

I had the pleasure of visiting Alexandria some years ago, when on my way to the Holy Land. The steamer which brought us from the south of Europe landed us at this famous city, as we wished to see the Pyramids and the Nile before entering Palestine. Some distance from the city were several famous obelisks, or large square columns, each made of a single block of stone sixty or seventy feet long, and tapering to the end like a pyramid. One of them was called Pompey's Pillar, and two are known as Cleopatra's Needles. These are very ancient, and strangers feel a great interest in visiting them. One of Cleopatra's Needles has been given to the English Government, and now stands on the bank of the river Thames; another was given to our country, and may be seen in the great Central Park of the city of New York.

In this city of Alexandria was the scene of the life and labours of Athanasius, one of the noblest heroes of the early Church, whose history we are now considering.

He is the only one of their number, except Basil, to whom the term *great* has been generally applied. He was justly entitled to it. He was not called upon, as many of those brave men were, to lay down his life as a martyr in defence of the truth of the Bible; but he had the privilege of spending all his days in supporting that truth in its purity, and of spreading it abroad in its power.

The parents of Athanasius were intelligent Christians, and he had, from his earliest years, the advantage of the best possible training and instruction. Cave, the well-known English writer, to whom we are indebted for the best history of the lives of the apostolic fathers, gives an interesting incident that took place in connection with Athanasius when he was a boy. On one occasion a company of eight or ten boys, from seven or eight to twelve or thirteen years old, were playing on the shore of the Mediterranean Sea. Athanasius was among them, and he was the oldest of the company. Alexander, the bishop of the church in that town, and whose house stood upon the shore near where the boys were, was waiting for some of his clergy who had been invited to dine with him. While waiting thus, he was interested in watching the boys on the shore. He found to his surprise that they were playing church. Athanasius had been appointed their bishop. Two of the next older boys were acting as ministers. Three of the younger boys, who had never been baptized, were brought forward as candidates for baptism. The service was gone through with as orderly and solemnly as though they had really been in church. At the close of the service the verse of a hymn was sung, and the benediction pronounced by the boy-bishop, and the congregation went home.

After Alexander the bishop had entertained his clerical friends at dinner, he sent for Athanasius and had a talk with him; and finding that he had not done this for mere sport, but because of the great interest he felt in religion and of his earnest desire to become a minister, Alexander sent for the father of Athanasius, and urged him to have his son educated for the ministry. He was accordingly put through the most complete and thorough education to fit him for that high office. He was only twenty-three years of age when he was ordained to the ministry and entered on its sacred duties. We do not know how long he was engaged in the studies which were to prepare him for the ministry. In my own case it took ten years; and if Athanasius was anything like as long as that in his preparation, then he must have been very young when he began his Christian life. And in every age of the Church's history the most active and useful men have always been those who began to serve God when they were young. We see this in the case of the good men of whom we read in the Bible. There were Joseph, and Moses, and Samuel, and David, and Josiah, and Jeremiah, and Daniel, and John the Baptist, and Timothy. These were among the most useful and honoured servants of God that the Church has ever known; and they all began to serve God early. Athanasius did the same;

and he made careful and earnest preparation for his life-work by much study of the Scriptures. When this was finished, the bishop took him into his own family as his private secretary ; and when Athanasius had reached his twenty-third year, he ordained him to the ministry, and had him engaged as his assistant in the work of the church of which he had charge.

Here we have the introduction of Athanasius to that important life-work in which he was occupied for more than half a century ; and in studying his history through all those years, we shall see how well he deserved to be called Athanasius the Great. There are four points of view from which we may contemplate this greatness.

1. He was great *in his defence of the truth.* Only six years after he had been ordained to the ministry, the Council of Nice was summoned by the emperor Constantine. It was to take action in regard to the erroneous teaching of Arius, who had denied the divinity of Christ, and was teaching that fatal error wherever he went.

A great many members of the Church, as well as ministers and bishops, were led away by these wrong views about the nature and character of our Saviour, Jesus Christ. They admitted that he was a good man, but they did not believe that he was God. This was fearful. If Jesus is not a divine being—if he is not the only begotten Son of God, equal to the Father in all things—then his death never could have atoned for our sins; he never could have made us righteous before God by anything that he has done for us; and then the gospel would lose all its power and preciousness.

But Athanasius was not led away by these errors. He studied the Scriptures diligently, with earnest prayer that God would help him to understand the truth. God heard his prayer and helped him; and the result was that, in an age of abounding error, he had a clear and intelligent understanding of the truth as it is in Jesus. He had so much to say about the doctrine of the Trinity, and said it so clearly and so boldly, that he has always been regarded as the great champion of this important doctrine. His name has been connected with one of the creeds used by the Church of England, which is called the " Athanasian Creed," not because he was the author of it, but because he was so brave a defender of the doctrines which it contains.

Three hundred and eighteen bishops were present at the Council of Nice. Alexander, bishop of Alexandria, was among those who attended. He took Athanasius with him, because he was clear and decided in his views of the doctrine in question, and because he knew he would be very useful in setting forth and upholding the teachings of Scripture on this important subject.

There were three parties present at that council. One was made up of those who held the orthodox

Trinitarian view respecting Christ. They believed that he was not only the Son of God, but was a partaker of the same nature with the Father. The second party was composed of the Arians, who denied the doctrine altogether. The third party was made up of those whose views were not clear on this subject, and who wished to form a creed which should be so expressed that both the other parties, the orthodox and the Arians, would be willing to sign it. The great controversy in that council had reference to this point. But the orthodox party were not willing to do this. They felt perfectly satisfied that the doctrine in question was a matter of too great importance to be expressed in a doubtful or uncertain way. While this controversy was going on, there was no one present in the council who had clearer views on this subject, or who expressed them more strongly, than Athanasius. He never would listen for a moment to any other statement of this doctrine than that which was set forth in the Nicene Creed. This declares that Christ is not only a divine being, but that he is a partaker of *the same nature* with the Father. And so the important matter was settled in this very way. Then the views of Arius on this subject were condemned by the council, while Arius himself was deposed from the ministry and sent into banishment.

The stand which Athanasius took on this subject at the council, he maintained unflinchingly through all the days of his life. Many of those who signed the creed then adopted afterwards changed their views, and signed a creed more favourable to the Arians; but Athanasius never would do this.

Not long after the Council of Nice, Alexander, the bishop of the church in Alexandria, died, and Athanasius was elected to be his successor. This was an occasion of great joy to his friends in that city. They felt sure that he was just the man for the position, and that as he had done so much to secure the adoption of the Nicene Creed, he would be most faithful in helping to maintain and defend the views expressed in it. And this is just what he did.

A few years after the Council of Nice, the emperor Constantine was persuaded by the friends of Arius to issue a decree for his release from banishment, his return to Alexandria his former place of abode, and for his entrance again upon the work of the ministry there. Then the emperor wrote to Athanasius, ordering him to receive Arius again into the communion of the Church. In answer to this letter, Athanasius told the emperor that under no circumstances whatever would he receive into the Church one who had been condemned by the Council of Nice for denying the divinity of the blessed Saviour. And when the emperor said that he must either receive Arius again into the Church or resign his office of bishop and go into banishment, Athanasius showed his greatness in the defence of the truth by giving up his high office and going into banishment.

2. Athanasius was great *in the trials through which he passed* in support of the truth. He was thirty years old when he was chosen to be bishop of the church in Alexandria. He retained that office for forty-six years. During that time he was on five different occasions driven into banishment. These banishments took up altogether twenty years of that part of his life in which the office of head of the church of Alexandria of right belonged to him. The cause of all these changes and the trouble resulting from them was found in the Arian controversy. Nothing could lead him for a moment to think of changing his views, or of giving up what he knew to be the truth about these things. No matter how many persons held different views from himself on this great subject, neither their number nor their power made any difference to him. He was earnest in holding on to the truth. In one of the controversies held on this subject, his adversaries told him that the world was against him. " Very well," said he ; " then let it be known that Athanasius is against the world." There was something noble in this. Athanasius's love for the truth connected with the character and work of Christ as taught in the Scriptures, his unfaltering defence of that truth, and his unwillingness to show any sympathy with those who denied it, led the members of the Arian party to be untiring in their persecution of him. Every time that he returned from banishment, his friends in

Alexandria would rejoice and be exceeding glad over the event; but his enemies the Arians would begin again to plot for his removal once more. They would make all sorts of false accusations against him to the emperor, charging him with fraud and dishonesty and immorality, and even murder. And they would never rest from these efforts till he was once more under sentence of banishment or threatened with death. At one time he would be sent to a strange city, now in one direction, and then in another; at another time he would be sent into the desert; and the last time he was driven from home, in his old age, he had to hide himself in his father's tomb outside of the city, and there he lived alone for months. Out of the forty-six years in which he was bishop, twenty were spent in exile from his home and friends, living in the desert or other strange places. And yet, notwithstanding all the suffering thus brought upon him, the thought of giving up the truth he had been taught never entered his mind. He went steadily on in the midst of all these trials and persecutions,—a splendid example of persevering piety. He never allowed anything to interfere with the work he had to do for God and for his fellow-men; and it is those who learn to persevere who meet with the most success in life. How trying such an experience of life must have been! and how nobly the greatness of his character comes out to view when we remember that all these long years of trouble came upon him simply as the result of his unfaltering faithfulness in standing up for the truth as it is in Jesus! In this view of his character how well he deserves to be called Athanasius the Great!

3. We see his greatness *in the way in which he bore his trials.* He never gave way to repining or fault-finding in the experience of them. When obliged again and again to leave his home and the church he so much loved, and go among strangers or to the solitary desert, he always resolved it into the will of God, and went on his way sustained and cheered by an unfaltering trust that God never makes a mistake, but orders all things wisely and well for his people. He had learned when trouble came to look up with confidence to his Father in heaven, and say, "Thy will be done." And then he waited patiently for the Lord's time to come, when the way would open for him to return to his home and friends and church again. If his place of banishment was a foreign city, he would strive in various ways to make himself useful to those about him there. If he was sent into the desert, he would seek out some cave or sheltered corner as his place of abode, and there would occupy himself in writing on the subjects of controversy which engaged the thoughts of Christian people in those days. Here are two incidents which illustrate the spirit in which he met the perils that surrounded him.

On one occasion the Arians, with a company of

soldiers, surrounded the church in which Athanasius had met his congregation for the purpose of celebrating the Lord's Supper with them. Leaving part of their force outside of the church, the soldiers entered with drawn swords, and began to slaughter the people on the right hand and on the left. Shrieks and screams filled the church. Athanasius was sitting calmly in his chair near the pulpit. Perfectly unmoved by the terrible sight, he called on one of the deacons to sing the One Hundred and Thirty-sixth Psalm. The deacon sang the first part of the verse, "O give thanks unto the Lord," and Athanasius and those about him joined in the chorus—"for his mercy endureth for ever." After singing a few verses, as the soldiers were coming forward, the clergy and friends about him urged him to leave the church. Rising from his chair, he said he would not stir a step till they went out. Then they formed a circle around him, and managed to get him safely out from the end of the church which they occupied.

On another occasion, the emperor Julian — who had once been a professing Christian, but had apostatized and gone back to the worship of the heathen gods—sent an order to the governor of Egypt to have Athanasius driven from Alexandria and from Egypt. When this was known, his friends gathered around him and began to lament with loud cries and tears. But Athanasius said, "Be of good cheer, my friends. Let us give way a little. This is but a small cloud,

and will soon blow over." After this he took a boat
and began to sail up the Nile towards the desert.
He had no sooner gone than an officer with some
soldiers went in pursuit to take him prisoner. When
they learned which way he had gone, they went after
him. His friends at home sent him word of this.
On receiving this message, the friends in the boat
with him tried to persuade him to go ashore and get
out of their way. " No," he replied; " let us rather
go and meet our executioner, that he may know that
greater is He that is with us than he that is against
us." Then he ordered the steersman to turn the boat
and go back towards Alexandria. Soon after, the
officer and his soldiers came up to them. He did not
know Athanasius, and never imagined that he would
be going back to Alexandria. He only inquired if
they had seen Athanasius. They said, " Yes; he is
not far off." Thus they got safely back to Alexandria;
and then Athanasius concealed himself till this storm
passed over, which it did in a little while. Many
other instances might be given showing how Athanasius escaped perils.

4. We see his greatness *in the amount of good he
did.* He did great good with his writings. These
were very numerous. A list of between fifty and
sixty of his works has come down to us. I do not
mean that he wrote this number of volumes. He did
write some volumes. He wrote a volume containing
a commentary on the Psalms, and one on the Incarna-

tion, and several others. But the rest of his writings were letters or sermons on different matters of doctrine and practice which bore on the controversies of that age. These were just what the Church then needed, and were eminently useful. His writings were all clear, strong, eloquent, and persuasive. He was not satisfied with any amount of mere argument in handling a subject that was before him; but his constant aim was to settle every point on the clear testimony of Scripture. And this was one thing that helped to make his writings so useful. A leading clergyman of his time, in writing to a young man who was studying for the ministry, said, " If you ever meet with anything that Athanasius has written, take a copy of it at once; and if you have no paper on which to transcribe it, write the chief points of it on some part of your dress."

And then not by his writings only, but by his words and actions, Athanasius made himself useful to all about him. One of the leading writers of his age thus speaks of him : " He was humble in his mind, as he was sublime in his life. He was a man of the noblest virtue, and yet so kind and gentle that any one might speak freely to him. He had so governed himself that his life was a continuous sermon; and his sermons never needed any corrections. All ranks and conditions of men could find something in him to admire and imitate. He was a comfort to the sorrowing, a staff to the aged, a guide to the young, and a benefactor to the poor. He was a friend to the widow, a father to the fatherless, a shelter to the stranger, a physician to the sick ; and, as the apostle said, ' he became all things to all men, that he might gain the more.' He was considered by those who knew him as the model of what a minister of Christ should be. He was a light to all about him, a pillar of faith, a second John the Baptist." That was what the men of his generation thought of him. He stood amidst the floods of strife and contention then prevailing as unmoved as the solid rock stands while the waves of the sea are dashing upon it. And when we think of Athanasius in defence of the truth, in the peculiar trials he had to bear, in the spirit in which he met these trials, and in his wonderful usefulness, we see how he may well be called Athanasius the Great.

XII.

Julian the Apostate.

Born a.d. 331; Died a.d. 363.

THE well-known person of whom we are now to speak was not one of the heroes of the Church. He might have become a hero; instead, he was an enemy of the Church, and tried hard to effect its overthrow. He lived at the same time with Athanasius, of whom we wrote in the former chapter. It is because he was once a professor of the Christian religion, and then became one of the most bitter and wicked opposers of the truth which the heroes were spreading, that we speak of him here. His course was a very singular one, and the lessons we may learn from his history are striking and profitable.

Let us glance briefly at the leading facts of Julian's life, and then consider three suggestive lessons taught us by those facts.

Julian is called "the Apostate" because, although he was brought up in the Christian religion, and made a profession of his faith in it while young, yet when he was made emperor he renounced Christianity and became a worshipper of the old heathen gods, and tried to destroy the religion of Christ.

Julian was born in the year 331, and died from a wound received in a battle with the Persians in the year 363. He was a nephew of that distinguished man Constantine the Great, who was the first Christian emperor that Rome ever had. He spent his early years in the earnest and diligent study of poetry and philosophy, and other branches of education, in several of the most famous seats of learning, and especially at the university of Athens. He was a man of pleasing manners and of excellent morality.

He was proclaimed Emperor of Rome in 361, when he was just thirty years of age. He set himself at once earnestly to the work of reopening the old heathen temples and restoring the worship of Jupiter and other gods. His purpose was to overturn the Christian religion; and how far he might have succeeded in carrying out this object had his life been prolonged no one can tell, but before he had reigned two years he met his death as we have already described. And now let us look at the lessons taught us by his life.

1. We see illustrated, in the history of Julian the Apostate, *the loss a child sustains who does not have a pious, loving mother to mould his character.*

This is something which Julian never had. His mother died when he was but a few months old. A mother's love and a mother's care were blessings he did not know. If he had only been blessed with a mother's voice to instruct him and a mother's hand to direct his steps, how different the history of his life might have been !

"It is a well-known fact," says one, "that the most distinguished men who have adorned the Church by their virtues, or who have served their country by their noble actions, have been men who had enjoyed the privilege of receiving from pious mothers the high-toned principles of morality and duty by which they were influenced."

The mother of our great and good Washington was a shining example of piety and purity, and we see those virtues reproduced in her illustrious son. John Quincy Adams's mother was distinguished for her intelligence and piety, and her son said, "I owe all I am to my mother." The mother of John Wesley was remarkable for her intelligence, piety, and active ability, and she is justly called "the mother of Methodism." Benjamin West, that distinguished artist, ascribed his renown to his mother's kiss. When quite young, he drew a sketch of his little baby sister asleep in her cradle. In that rough outline his mother saw the evidence of genius, and in her maternal pride she kissed her son. In after life West used to say, "That kiss made me an artist." Let me say to the readers of these pages, "My young friends, if you are blessed with a pious mother, thank God for it. Listen to her words ; obey and honour her." If Julian had been blessed with such a mother, and had minded her, he never would have been known as the Apostate.

2. We see illustrated, in the history of Julian, *the importance of having a good foundation on which to build our religious character.*

Julian did not have such a foundation. He never really learned to know and love the Saviour. His heart was never changed, and he knew not what it was to be made a new creature in Christ Jesus. And so he was just like the man of whom our Saviour speaks in the parable (Matt. vii. 26, 27), who built his house on the sand, without a foundation. When the rain descended, and the winds blew, and the floods came, and beat upon that house, it fell; and great was the fall of it. And it was just so with Julian. He built the house of his Christian profession on the sand. He had no proper foundation for it to stand on; and when Satan tempted him to give up his religion, he did so, and then indeed the ruin of his house was great. It caused the failure of his plans for life. In addition to this, he lost his soul by it, and this was to lose everything.

In building up the house of our religious character, let us be sure that we get down to the solid rock and find a good foundation there. I mean by this that we should learn truly to know and love Jesus and have our hearts changed by him. This is the true foundation on which to build. If we build here we are safe. No matter how the rain descends, or the winds blow, or the floods come, our house will never fall, because it is built on the "Rock of ages." No matter how much Satan may tempt us, we shall never turn our back on Jesus and become apostates like Julian. Jesus said to his disciples, "My sheep shall never perish, neither shall any *man* pluck them out of my hand" (John x. 27, 28). Let us be sure that we really know and love Jesus; for thus we become his sheep, and then we are safe for ever, in spite of all that Satan or any of our enemies can do.

3. We find illustrated, in Julian's history, *the folly of setting ourselves against the plans and purposes of God.*

When Julian renounced the religion of Christ, and made up his mind to establish the old heathen religion in the place of it, he was setting himself deliberately and decidedly against the purpose of God. And what was the result? It was just what might have been expected. Job asks the question, "Who hath hardened *himself* against him, and hath prospered?" (Job ix. 4.)

Two events in the life of Julian may be referred to as illustrating the truth of Job's words. One of these was what he undertook to do at Jerusalem. He knew that the purpose of God was to have that city and its temple remain in ruins; but he made up his mind to upset that purpose, and have Jerusalem rebuilt. In trying to do this he caused great quantities of materials of various kinds to be collected together, and committed the carrying out of this plan to an agent of his. The Jews of course heartily supported this work. Even their women took part in it, carrying off the earth which covered the temple in the laps of their garments. But the work, we are told, was suddenly stopped in a marvellous way by means of a fire, a whirlwind, and an earthquake. The buildings in process of erection were thrown down; many persons perished in this way, and the undertaking was abandoned.

The other event which illustrates the point of the subject now before us is seen in the way in which the life of Julian was brought to an end. We are told that when he started on his last expedition into Persia, he said to some of his friends, " I will go and put an end to this war in Persia; and then I will come back and overturn the religion of Christ."

He went on that journey; but in one of the first battles with the Persians an arrow pierced his side. It soon became manifest that this wound would cause his death; and as he lay bleeding there, we are told that he took a bowl in his hand, let the blood from his wound flow into it, and then, throwing the contents of the bowl towards heaven, exclaimed, " Thou hast conquered, O thou Galilean ! " Thus Julian died, in the thirty-second year of his age. Disappointment and death were the result which came to Julian from setting himself against the plans and purposes of God; and a similar experience is all that can be expected by any who follow his example. We cannot prosper when we try to do what is contrary to the will of God. Unhappiness, disappointment, and ruin must be the result in every such case. Then let us resolve never to tread in Julian's footsteps in this respect. The only safe and wise thing for each of us to do is to obey the voice which comes to us from God's word, saying, " Acquaint now thyself with him, and be at peace ; thereby good shall come unto thee " (Job xxii. 21).

XIII.

Basil the Great.

BORN A.D. 329 (?) ; DIED A.D. 379 (?).

BASIL is the next hero that comes before us in the catalogue of the good men whose history we are studying. Basil was born at Cæsarea, in Palestine, in the year 329; and died there in 379, when he was only about fifty years old. He never was very strong in health, and the earnestness with which he entered upon and prosecuted the important duties that devolved upon him in connection with the Church had much to do with the shortening of his days. He was connected, on the side both of his father and mother, with ancient and very honourable families. His father had occupied very distinguished positions both in the army and the government of his country. He was also a man of great piety, and had done much, both by his labours and his sufferings, to build up and defend the cause of Christianity. Basil's parents had ten children, of whom he was the oldest. His father, after whom he was named, his mother Emmelia, and his grandmother Macerina, who were all earnest Christians, united together in giving him, from his earliest childhood, the most careful Christian education. They sowed the seed of Scriptural truth in his mind and heart ; and the seed thus sown took root, sprang up, and bore abundant fruit, to their joy, to the good of others, and to the glory of God.

Basil acted a very important part in the history of the Church in the latter part of the fourth century of our era. The title of " Great " was given to him— he is always spoken of as Basil the Great—and he well deserved this title. We may speak of four things in connection with him which show him to have been really great.

1. He was *great in his learning.* Cæsarea was famous for its schools and institutions of learning. Basil went through all of them, one after another. Then he went to Constantinople. This had been made the imperial city of the eastern empire. Some of the most distinguished professors of philosophy that were in the world were to be found there. Basil availed himself of those rare advantages. He learned all that those great men could teach in their several departments. Then he went to Athens. This had long been known as the most celebrated seat of learning to be found in the world. Here he had the best opportunity of finding out all that could be known about grammar, rhetoric, philosophy, arithmetic, geometry, mathematics, astronomy, history, languages, and every branch of human learning. And when his mind

was enriched by all these boundless stores of human knowledge, he devoted himself to the careful and diligent study of the Scriptures. When we think of him, on the one hand, as taught by God's blessed Spirit, and then, on the other hand, as having all these boundless stores of knowledge from which to draw his illustrations of the great truths of the Bible, we can easily understand what a blessed influence for good he must have exerted as a teacher and defender of the Word of God. Among all the ministers of the Church in his day there were none to be compared with him. He made use of his great learning by engaging in earnest controversy with the Arians and all the other teachers of heresy. He was able so clearly to point out the errors which they taught, that they were afraid to meet him in argument. They could not answer the clear, strong statements which he made in pointing out their erroneous teachings. And when he stood boldly forth in defence of the great truths of the Bible, the false teachers of those days would flee before him, just as the Philistines fled after David had vanquished Goliath, the great Philistine giant, who stood forth and defied any in Israel to meet him in battle. And when we think of this hero of the early Church standing, as he did, head and shoulders above all the men of his generation in this respect, we do not wonder when we hear him spoken of as Basil the Great. He was great in his learning.

2. Basil was *great in his piety.* We see his great piety in the simplicity and self-denial of his life. His manner of living was of the very plainest possible character. He seemed always to remember what Jesus said of himself, " The foxes have holes, and the birds of the air have nests, but the Son of man hath not where to lay his head." And though our Saviour did not leave any command to his disciples to live in the same way, yet Basil seemed to think that it was right for the disciple not to be above his Master, nor the servant above his Lord. He wanted to have the same mind that was in Christ Jesus, to tread in the blessed steps of his most holy life, and as far as possible to live and act just as he lived and acted. The house that Basil lived in was one of the very plainest kind. He never allowed himself to have more than one coat at a time, and that he wore without any ornament. He did not feel that there was any merit in doing this ; it was simply the feeling of piety ruling in his heart which led him thus to live. As he called himself a disciple or follower of Jesus, he wished to be as nearly like him in his manner of living as it was possible for him to be. He knew that Jesus had said, " If any man will be my disciple, let him deny himself, and take up his cross daily, and follow me." And this was what he aimed to do ; and so we see the great piety of Basil in the simplicity and self-denial of his daily life.

3. We see his great piety again in *his practical*

charity. His father was a rich man. Before his death he divided his property among his ten children. There was enough to make each of them well off. When Basil entered upon his religious life, he set apart a large portion of his inheritance for the relief of the suffering poor; and in the year 359, when a great famine was prevailing, he sold all the rest of his property, and used the money which it brought him in the same way. And when he had given away all that belonged to himself, and the wants of the poor were unsupplied, he appealed to the rich members of the church under his charge, and continued his efforts till he had opened first their hearts and then their purses, and all the money needed for the relief of the poor was freely furnished. Then he gathered together the famishing poor of both sexes and all ages, and distributed freely to them the food which they needed. After this, by the help of his friends, he had a large hospital built outside of the city. Into this he gathered the sick, the lame, the blind, the aged, who were unable to take care of themselves. There they were carefully nursed, and all their wants were provided for. He cheerfully assisted in this work himself, and was ever ready to perform the humblest offices for the poor sufferers found there. Surely this was a satisfactory proof of his great piety.

And then we have another proof of piety in the faithful way in which he gave up the pursuits and pleasures of the world when he became a follower of Christ. He renounced the pomps and vanities of the world when he joined the Church. He felt sure that the world and the Church cannot be joined together. They constitute two masters, and no man can serve them both. In taking Christ as his Master he determined that the world should no longer lead or control him. He believed the truth of the apostle's words when he said, " If any man love the world, the love of the Father is not in him." When we make a profession of religion, we solemnly promise " to renounce the devil and all his works, the pomps and vanities of this wicked world, and that we will not follow nor be led by them." How Christians who go to balls and theatres, and engage freely in worldly amusements, can reconcile their conduct with the apostle's words above quoted I never can understand. Basil had no sympathy with such Christians. One way in which he showed his great piety was by heartily renouncing all worldly pursuits and pleasures.

4. He was *great in his usefulness.* After he had gone through with his studies in the different places of which we have spoken, he returned to Cæsarea, his native place, and was occupied for several years as a lawyer. In this he was eminently successful. But he soon grew tired of such employment. It did not suit his earnest Christian character. Then he retired to a mountainous part of the country and established a monastery. There he devoted himself to prayer

and fasting and diligent study. He had a number of young men who joined him there, and whom he prepared for the work of the ministry. After several years spent in this way he returned to Cæsarea. Then he was ordained to the ministry, and engaged earnestly in every kind of Christian work, till the year 369, when Eusebius, the bishop of the church of Cæsarea, died, and Basil was chosen to be his successor. And in occupying these different positions, we can see how useful he was in three ways.

(1.) *He was useful in what he said.* Whether he was visiting the sick and poor from house to house, or preaching from the pulpit or by the wayside, he had but one subject about which to speak, and that was, " Jesus Christ, and him crucified." And this great theme he handled with wonderful power. He was the most eloquent preacher of the age in which he lived. The emperor Constans was so charmed with the eloquence of his preaching that he had a life-size statue of brass erected to his honour in Rome, on the base of which was this inscription :—

ROME, THE QUEEN OF CITIES, TO BASIL, THE KING OF ELOQUENCE.

A well-known writer of that day, in speaking of him, says : " In his own peculiar way, he so adapted himself to popular audiences that he never spoke anything but what the most ignorant among them could understand, and yet the most learned would admire. The truth is," continues the same writer, "that if in anything he excelled all other speakers, it was in his eloquence." And when we think of him as going about teaching and preaching in such a way, who can tell how useful he was in what he said ?

(2.) *He was useful also in what he did.* What he taught with his eloquent voice he illustrated in his holy life. His preaching and his practising were in beautiful harmony. It might well have been said of him that the same mind was in him that was also in Christ Jesus. Humility and patience and gentleness and love were the chief features that marked his character. He won the respect and confidence of all who knew him. And he was untiring in his efforts to promote the growth and prosperity of the Church. When he was chosen to the high office which he held as head of the church at Cæsarea and the surrounding country, he went everywhere, visiting the different churches, giving wise counsel and advice to the ministers, and seeking to correct whatever was wrong in the habits and practices of the people ; and in this way, like his blessed Master, he "went about doing good."

And then he stood bravely and nobly up in defence of the truth. When the emperor and the principal officers of the government had joined the Arian party, and tried to secure his influence in support of their erroneous views, he never would yield to their wishes in any way, but stood firm as a rock in support and defence of the great truth respecting the divinity of Christ, and the atonement he had offered for the sins of the world. And so, by defending the truths of the Bible, and in helping to spread them abroad on the right hand and on the left, he was eminently useful in what he did.

Finally: *he was also useful in what he wrote.* He wrote commentaries on different portions of Scripture, sermons on various Christian duties, essays against the errors of the Arians and other leading heretics, and letters on many of the most important subjects which engaged the attention of the members of the Church in those days; and the writings of his pen seemed to have the same charm and power that marked the utterances of his voice. One of the leading ministers of the Church in the time of Basil speaks thus of his writings: "When I read his expositions of Scripture, I seem to be conversing with my great Creator, and feel a greater reverence and admiration for him than ever I did before. When I read his work on the Holy Spirit, I feel myself in the presence of the true God, and, embracing the views there given, I feel better prepared to preach and declare the truth of God than ever I was before. And when I read his sermons for the poor and the ignorant, I find myself transported beyond the mere letter of the words, and carried up from one degree of light to another, and feel changed into another being."

And when we think of this good man with reference to what he said and what he did and what he wrote, we do not wonder to find how very useful he was. May God give us all grace to follow him as he followed Christ!

XIV.

Ambrose of Milan.

BORN 340 (?); DIED 397 (?).

A MBROSE comes next in our list of Christian
heroes, and he is most worthy of the place he
occupies among them. In going on to consider the
character of Ambrose, there are three things of which
to speak. These are, *the leading incidents of his history, the scene of his labours*, and *the lessons of usefulness illustrated in his life*.

1. *The leading incidents of his history.* He was
born in the town of Arles, in France, in the year 340
of our era, and died at Milan in the year 397, when
he was in the fifty-seventh year of his age. His
father was a distinguished man, and governor of one
of the western provinces of the Roman empire. Arles
was his residence while exercising the office of prefect or governor of that part of the empire, and it
was while he resided there that Ambrose was born.
He was nursed and brought up in the palace which
belonged to the governor. One day, as he lay asleep
in his cradle in the open court, it is said that a swarm

of bees settled on his face, gently creeping in and out
of his open mouth without hurting him.   His father,
who was passing by, saw it.   He told the nurse not
to drive them away, for it was a sign that the child
would become a great man and an eloquent speaker.
His father did not live long after this.   Then his
mother removed with her family to Rome, where
Ambrose was brought up.   His mother was an earnest Christian, and from her he received a thoroughly
religious education.

Ambrose made up his mind to be a lawyer, and
was trained for that profession by passing through
the best schools existing in Rome.   He was very successful as a lawyer, and gained the confidence and
respect of all who knew him.   After practising law
for several years, he was appointed by the representa-
tive of the emperor to the office of proconsul or governor of the northern part of Italy.   In taking leave
of him, his friend who had procured this honourable
position for him said, " Now go thy way, and govern
more like a bishop than a judge."

After this Ambrose made Milan his residence ; and
here he was so faithful in the discharge of his duties,
and so kind and pleasing in his manners, that he became very popular among the people of that city.
After he had been there about five years, Auxentius,
the bishop of the church in Milan, died.   Soon after
this a council of the church was called for the purpose of electing a successor to Auxentius.   He had

been an Arian, and his friends desired to elect some one of the same views ; but to this the orthodox portion of the council would not consent. This led to a fierce and angry controversy. The longer they argued the matter, the less prospect there was of their coming to any agreement. When Ambrose heard how things were going in the council, he went there and asked permission to say a few words. This was granted him. Then he made an earnest and eloquent speech, exhorting them to lay aside their contentions, and, in the peaceful spirit which their religion taught, to unite in making choice of a proper person to fill the important office that was vacant. His speech made a profound impression on the council. For a time there was perfect silence ; then some one rose and moved that Ambrose should be chosen bishop. The motion was taken up at once and carried unanimously. How strange this was ! Ambrose was not then a minister ; he had not even joined the church ; but he was an earnest Christian man, and was then preparing to be baptized. This is probably the only case in the history of the Church when one not a minister, but a layman and a lawyer, was chosen to be a bishop.

Ambrose was unwilling to accept this high and holy office. He withdrew from the city, and got a friend who lived some miles away to let him stay in retirement in his dwelling. But the emperor issued a proclamation requiring any person who knew where he was to make it known, and threatening a severe penalty for detaining or hiding him. Then he returned to Milan, and was made bishop of the church there. These are the incidents in the history of Ambrose of which we wished to speak.

2. *The scene of his labours.* The famous city of Milan was the place in which he exercised his ministry for twenty-two years, and faithfully discharged his duties as the head of the church there. Milan was the capital of Lombardy and the principal city of northern Italy. It stands within easy reach of the beautiful lakes of Maggiore and Como and the river Po. It has a population of nearly two hundred thousand inhabitants, and is justly regarded as one of the pleasantest cities of Europe. It has many famous palaces and public buildings; but these are all cast in the shade by its magnificent cathedral. Next to St. Peter's at Rome, this is the largest and most beautiful cathedral in Italy. It stands in the centre of the city. It is built of white marble, and has a very imposing appearance. I never shall forget the intense pleasure I felt while standing and gazing at it. The erection of this building was begun in 1386—over five hundred years ago—and it is not finished yet. The workmen have little huts on the marble roof of the cathedral, and spend their days there. There are nearly five thousand life-size marble statues of distinguished men in the niches and corners of this vast building; and yet its size is such that this great crowd can hardly be seen. And it was the city which has

since been adorned with this splendid cathedral that
was the field in which Ambrose laboured.

3. *The lessons of usefulness with which we are furnished in the life of Ambrose.*

We may look at his usefulness from three points of
view :—(1.) We see it in *what he did to increase interest in the public worship of God.*   Ambrose had a great
talent for music, and an unusual ability for teaching
others in it.   He was a great blessing to the church
in the hymns which he wrote and in the music which
he introduced into the public worship of God.   Music
had been used in the sanctuary before his time, but
there was no proper form or order in the use of it.
Ambrose made a great improvement in this part of
the service of the sanctuary.   He arranged the hymns
and chants, with the music with which they were
sung, in such a way as added greatly to the interest
and profit of the worshippers.   A distinguished writer
of that day, after attending service in the cathedral
of Milan, speaks of its effect upon him in these words :
" The voices flowed into my ears, the truth sung
thrilled my heart, and tears of joy filled my soul, as I
listened to the sweet strains that sounded through the
sanctuary."   Ambrose lived in the fourth century of
the Christian era ; we are living in the nineteenth
century ; and here the interesting fact comes out that
for fifteen hundred years this good man has been a
blessing to the Church, in the efforts which he made
to improve the musical part of the worship of the

sanctuary.   Some of the hymns which he wrote are
still used in the Milan cathedral, with the music to
which he set them.   Here is one of them as it has
been translated into English :—

AN ANCIENT HYMN OF ST. AMBROSE.

Thou image of the Father bright !
Effulgent glory, Light of light,
Radiance divine, that shines for aye,
Thy dawn is that of endless day.

True Sun ! illume our inner sight ;
Pour down thy Spirit's living light ;
Through all our senses, o'er our head,
Unsetting Sun, thy brightness shed.

Father of lights ! on thee we call ;
Father of glory ! all in all,
Father of grace and power, we pray,
Put all our sin and guilt away.

Jesus ! be thou our bread from heaven ;
Let faith athirst for thee be given ;
Then let us drink with joy, until
Our hearts and souls thy Spirit fill.

Then glad the day we shall begin,
Blush with the morning for our sin,
Our faith grow like the mid-day bright,
But know no twilight and no night.

As dawn ascends to noon of day,
Be thou our rising Sun for aye ;
Thee let us in thy Father see,
And find the Father all in thee.   Amen.

There is one chant which has been used for ages in
the morning service of the Church of England and of
the Protestant Episcopal Church in this country, which
is called the Ambrosian chant, or the chant of Ambrose.   Its title is the " Te Deum," from the first two

words in the Latin version of it. Ambrose is said by some to have been the author of this chant, or the one who first brought it into use. By others it is affirmed that this chant was not used in the Church till several centuries after the death of Ambrose; so the question remains an unsettled one. But the name and memory of Ambrose are connected with it, and this makes it interesting. The first two verses of this chant read thus: " We praise thee, O God; we acknowledge thee to be the Lord. All the earth doth worship thee, the Father everlasting;" and those who use this chant in the worship of the sanctuary must feel something inspiring in it when they think of the multitudes now in heaven who for century after century have repeated its solemn words through all the days of their pilgrimage. And here we see how useful Ambrose was in what he did to add to the interest and profitableness of the public worship of God.

(2.) We see the usefulness of Ambrose in *his faithful defence of the truth.* The controversy with the Arians was still kept up with great warmth. They had no church in Milan, and were very anxious to have one. Justina, the wife of the emperor, was an Arian. At the request of the leading men of that party she made application to Ambrose to allow them the use of one of the churches in the city. But Ambrose refused to do this. He said that the office intrusted to him as the head of the church required him to be faithful in upholding and defending the

truth which God had revealed in his holy Word, and
therefore he could not allow any of the churches
under his care to be used by those who denied the
divinity of his blessed Master and the reality of the
atonement which he had made. Then Justina persuaded her husband, the emperor, to issue a decree
commanding that one of the churches of the city
should be given to the Arians for their use, and
threatening with imprisonment and death any persons
who should interfere with the carrying out of this decree. Then a company of soldiers was sent to take
possession of the church which the Arians desired to
have. Ambrose was in that church, standing near the
pulpit, when the soldiers entered. The officer of the
company came up to him and said that he had been
commanded by the emperor to take possession of the
church for the use of the Arians. "Go back to the
emperor," said Ambrose, "and tell him that if he
wishes any money or property belonging to me, he is
welcome to it. If he wishes to take my life, I will
yield it to him cheerfully. But this church belongs to
God. It has been committed to my care, and while I
live I never can allow it to be used by those who deny
the truth respecting the character and work of Christ
as God has revealed it to us in his Word." These
words of Ambrose had such an effect upon the emperor
that he would not pursue the matter any further;
and so the Arians failed to secure the church which
they wished.

There are other incidents in the life of this good man which illustrate equally well his faithfulness in defending the truth. Let us all try to understand the saving truth of the gospel as Ambrose understood it, and let us stand up faithfully in its defence as he did, and then, in our measure, we shall be useful as he was.

(3.) Ambrose was useful in *the practical illustrations of the truth* which are furnished in his life. He was the model of a good Christian, a good minister, and a good bishop. He was so much beloved and reverenced by all who knew him that we do not wonder to find him generally spoken of as *Saint* Ambrose.

We have illustrated in his life *the lesson of humility.* We see this in the way in which he shrank from taking upon himself the office of the head of the church to which he had been unanimously chosen by the council of Milan. He felt unwilling to assume the duties and responsibilities of so important a position. And it was the honest feeling of his heart—his real humility—which made him so unwilling to accept that office. Ambrose had learned the lesson which Jesus came down from heaven to teach us. When he had washed his disciples' feet, to illustrate this lesson, he said to them, "If I then, your Lord and Master, have washed your feet; ye also ought to wash one another's feet." Let us all try to learn humility.

Again, we see *the lesson of self-denial* well illustrated in the life of Ambrose. When he was ordained to the ministry and made a bishop in the church, he gave up all the property belonging to him for the support of the church and the relief of the poor. And what he thus did at the beginning of his ministerial life he kept on doing to the end of it. He lived in the plainest, simplest way, and used all the money he could save for the purpose of doing good. We cannot be true Christians unless we learn and practise self-denial. Jesus made this point very clear when he said so solemnly, "If any man will come after me, let him deny himself, and take up his cross daily, and follow me." Ambrose learned this lesson well, and his whole life was a practical illustration of it.

And then again, in *the lesson of home piety* which his life illustrated, we see how useful Ambrose was. He loved the public service of the sanctuary. It was his delight to join in the praises of God as they were sung there. But when he returned from the sanctuary he did not leave his religion behind him; he carried it with him wherever he went, and it entered into everything he did. And this is just as it should be. That wise English minister, the Rev. Rowland Hill, used to say, "I would not give a straw for any man's religion unless his cat and dog are the better for it." He meant to say by this that when our religion is true and genuine it will make us faithful in every duty, and kind and gentle to all about us, even to the dumb creatures of God. Jesus "went about doing good;" and he expects all his people to follow his example in this respect. This was what Ambrose did. His practice conformed to his preaching. He loved to visit the homes of the poor, to comfort those who were in trouble, and to pray by the bedside of the sick and dying. And thus we see how useful he was in the practical illustrations of the truth which were found in his daily life. Let us all try to follow his example in these respects; and then we shall be useful wherever we go, and it will be true of us that we shall be " treading in the blessed steps of our Saviour's most holy life."

XV.

John Chrysostom.

Born a.d. 347 ; Died a.d. 407.

A MONG all the great and good men of that part
of the Church's history we are now considering
there were none possessed of nobler qualities, or who
exercised a greater influence for good, than the famous
man whose life and character we are now to consider.
He was born at Antioch in Syria in a.d. 347, and died
in 407, when in the sixtieth year of his age. His
name was John Chrysostom ; but the different titles
of Doctor, Bishop, Archbishop, and Saint were given
him by turns. The name of Chrysostom did not be-
long to his family ; it comes from a Greek word which
signifies " golden-mouthed," and was applied to him in
order to express the remarkable eloquence that belonged to him as a public speaker.

Antioch, the place of Chrysostom's birth, was a very
distinguished city. It was named after Antiochus
Epiphanes, by whom it was founded, and was considered the capital of Syria, being the residence of the
Syrian kings. As we have said in a former chapter, it

was beautifully situated on the river Orontes, and in full view of the Lebanon range of mountains. It ranked high among the most famous cities of that day. Rome was the first, Alexandria the second, and Antioch the third. It was a very populous city. In the days of Chrysostom it had a population of two hundred thousand inhabitants. He states that the church with which he was connected had under its care three thousand poor people, and provided for all their wants.

The father of Chrysostom was a distinguished officer in the army of his country, but he died very soon after the birth of his son. This left the care and education of him entirely in the hands of his mother. Her name was Arethusa. She was an earnest Christian woman. When her husband died she was left quite a young widow. She resolved, however, never to marry again, but to devote her life to the careful education of her dear child. By her example, her prayers, and her daily teaching, he was early brought to a knowledge of the truth and an experience of the grace and love of God. She secured for him the best teachers that were to be found in Antioch, which was then quite celebrated for its institutions of learning. There was then a very famous teacher of elocution in Antioch, whose name was Libanius; and though he was still a worshipper of idols, the mother of Chrysostom resolved that her son should have the benefit of his instruction. Then Chrysostom entered on this course of study with great interest, and there can be no doubt that this had much to do in helping to develop in him that unusual power of eloquence which in after life distinguished him as a public speaker.

When his preparatory education was finished, he first engaged for some time in the practice of a lawyer. But he soon became dissatisfied with this, and wished to retire to a monastery and devote some years of his life to the quiet and careful study of the Scriptures. His mother did not approve of this. She had a long and earnest conversation with him on the subject, and entreated him to give up this plan and to remain with her during the rest of her life, as she very much desired his help and presence. He yielded cheerfully to her request, and devoted himself lovingly to her comfort as long as she lived.

But after his mother's death, Chrysostom retired into private life, and lived in great simplicity and self-denial as a hermit. He devoted his time mainly to prayer and the diligent study of the Scriptures. After five or six years thus spent he returned to Antioch, and was ordained to the ministry, and devoted himself untiringly to the duties of that holy office. In A.D. 397 he was elected bishop of the church in Constantinople. He only occupied that position for about ten years. These were years of great trials and difficulties to him. His faithfulness in defending the true doctrines of the gospel made him many enemies among the Arians and other false teachers. They made false charges against him, and had him twice banished from his church at Constantinople. During the second of these banishments, while travelling to the distant place to which he had been sent, overcome by the fatigue of the journey, he was taken sick and died. These are the leading facts in the history of this good and great man.

And now, having made this statement, we may glance very briefly at some of the important lessons that we find illustrated in the life of Chrysostom.

1. We see his *earnest piety* illustrated in *the zealous labours which he performed.* As soon as he entered on the great work assigned him as the head of the church, he set himself vigorously to attend to it. He found that through the neglect of his predecessor in the high office of bishop, things had been allowed to get in a very bad way. Both the clergy and the lay members of the church had adopted practices and ways of living that were not at all in accordance with the teachings of Scripture. These Chrysostom set himself at once to correct, both by precept and by example. His own style of living was of the plainest and most self-denying character.

Chrysostom inherited a large amount of property from his father. This he consecrated to the Lord and employed in doing good among the poor. The church under his charge had a very large income. Out of this he took for himself only just enough to meet the expenses of the very simple way in which he lived. All the rest was employed in carrying on the good work in which the church was engaged.

Not long after entering on the important duties of his high office, he found, to his surprise, that there was a province not far from Constantinople where idolatry was still prevailing with all its attendant darkness and misery. He went to work at once, and had what we should call a missionary society formed for the purpose of evangelizing that portion of the country. He had money raised and missionaries sent out, and never ceased his efforts till idolatry was given up there, and the gospel of Jesus, with all its blessed influences, was spread abroad throughout that district.

2. Then, in his *patient suffering*, as well as in his zealous labours, we see his earnest piety illustrated. The empress Eudoxia, the wife of the emperor then reigning, was an Arian. She was very much offended at Chrysostom for his faithfulness in defending the teachings of Scripture as held by the Trinitarians. She would not rest till the emperor was persuaded to issue a decree for the banishment of Chrysostom from his church and country. This occasioned great distress and sorrow among the friends of the persecuted man. But he himself made no complaint about it, and offered no resistance to it. The patient spirit with which he submitted to all the suffering involved in his banishment, is seen in what he said about it when the decree was first made known to him. These are the words which he used on that occasion : " Well, the empress wishes to banish me.

Let her do it : yet the earth is the Lord's, and the fulness thereof. If she command that I be cut to pieces, let me be sawn asunder ; the prophet Isaiah was so served before me. Will she throw me into the sea ? I remember that was the fate of Jonah. Will she cast me into the fiery furnace ? Then I shall have the three children for my fellow-sufferers. If she cast me to the wild beasts, I know how Daniel went the same way to the lions. If she command that I be stoned, let it be so ; I shall then have Stephen, the proto-martyr, on my side. Will she have my head ? Let her take it ; John the Baptist lost his. Has she a mind for my estate ? Let her have it ; 'naked came I out of my mother's womb, and naked shall I return thither.'" And when death approached him during his second banishment, after taking leave of his friends and engaging in his last act of worship he clasped his hands on his breast and said, "Glory to God for all things that happen. Amen." And so he passed away. Surely such a patient spirit as this, in view of the great sufferings through which he was called to pass, was a good illustration of his earnest piety.

3. We see his *courage and faithfulness* illustrated in the trying scenes of his busy life. It was his courage and faithfulness in opposing error and defending the truth which led the empress to procure his banishment, as we have already seen.

But there was another occasion on which these

noble points of his character were brought fully into play. This was in connection with a famous general in the army, whose name was Gainas. He and his soldiers were all Arians. He asked the emperor to have one of the churches in Constantinople set apart for the Arians to worship in. The emperor made this request known to Chrysostom, and asked him to do what Gainas wanted. But he declined to do so. He said that he had been appointed the head of the church in order that he might watch over and protect the interests of the truth as it was revealed in the Scriptures; and that for him to set apart a church for the use of those who denied the divinity of the blessed Saviour would be failing in the solemn trust committed to him, and that he would rather lay down his life than neglect to discharge his duty in a matter of such great importance. This was really noble in him; and the courage and faithfulness which he thus displayed set him before us as an example which it would be well for us all to imitate.

And then, in connection with the history of this noble hero of the early Church, we are furnished with a striking illustration of *the way in which God's providence works.*

In one place in the Bible, when God wishes to show what an interest he feels in the treatment which his people receive from those about them, he says, " He that toucheth you, toucheth the apple of his eye " (Zech. ii. 8). And if we allow ourselves to injure or ill-treat any of God's servants, we may be sure that he will punish us for it. This was never more strikingly illustrated than in what happened to those who had been the enemies of Chrysostom. The chief of these was the empress Eudoxia. It was she who procured his banishment. About three months after his death she was suddenly seized with some internal complaint. This occasioned her terrible suffering, and soon put an end to her life. And within two or three years after the death of Chrysostom, nearly all of those who had joined in the false charges brought against him and had helped to secure his banishment were overtaken by some strange calamity. One of them fell from his horse, broke his leg, and died from the effect of the fall. Another lost his speech, and was confined to his bed till he died. Some died of dropsy, and some of gout which tortured the fingers that had signed his condemnation. These providential visitations were so remarkable that the friends of Chrysostom could not help wondering over them, and quoting as they did so the passage of Scripture which says, " Verily he is a God that judgeth in the earth " (Ps. lviii. 11).

And when we think of the many utterances of God's truth by this " golden-mouthed " preacher, and of his writings which have come down to us in thirteen large volumes, we may form some idea of the great amount of good which he accomplished. The Greek Church still uses a liturgy which is said to have been written by Chrysostom, though some affirm that it was not known till a century or more after his death. But in the service of the Church of England, and of the Episcopal Church in this country, there is a short prayer, beautiful and comprehensive, which is always used at the close of the morning and evening service, and which is called " A Prayer of St. Chrysostom." It reads thus: " Almighty God, who hast given us grace at this time to make our common supplications unto thee ; and dost promise that where two or three are gathered together in thy name, thou wilt grant their requests; fulfil now, O Lord, the desires and petitions of thy servants as may be most expedient for them ; granting us in this world knowledge of thy truth, and in the world to come life everlasting. Amen."

May God so give his grace to all the readers of this volume that they may have the same spirit which animated this noble hero of the early Church, and be able to tread in the steps of his most useful life.

XVI.

Jerome.

Born a.d. 340 (?); Died a.d. 430 (?).

THE history of this learned man comes before us now as the next subject that claims our attention in considering the Heroes of the early Church. He well deserves a place among these heroes, for he was one of the most learned and able of the fathers of the Latin Church. In considering the life of this famous man, we shall briefly state the leading facts of his history, and then refer to three important practical matters we find illustrated therein.

Jerome was born in the year 340 of the Christian era, at a town called Stridon, in Dalmatia. This town was entirely destroyed by the Goths towards the close of the fourth century, and no trace was left remaining by which it can now be identified. His parents were earnest Christians, and his early education was attended to by his father. Then he went to Rome and studied Greek and Latin, and rhetoric and philosophy, under the care of Donatus, one of the most famous teachers of that day. While at Rome, he was admitted to the Church by baptism, and decided to devote himself to the service of his God and Saviour. In the year 373, he set out on a journey to the East in company with three of his most intimate friends, and settled for a time at Antioch in Syria. While residing there he and two of his friends were taken with a severe attack of fever. His friends died, but he recovered, and became from that time more earnest and decided in his Christian life than ever he had been before. After this he retired to the desert of Chalcis, and spent four years in self-denying, penitential exercises, and in the diligent study of the Hebrew language. Then he returned to active life, and took an earnest part in the religious controversies of the day.

In the year 379, he was ordained to the ministry ; but he never took charge of any particular church, as he preferred the life of a travelling preacher and a diligent student. He was one of the most eloquent speakers of that day, and very famous for his great learning.

The great mistake of his life was in supposing that religion was designed to separate us from our fellow-men and lead us to spend our days in acts of fasting and self-denial, as monks and hermits were accustomed to do.

After visiting Constantinople and other prominent places, he returned to Rome, and became the secretary and warm friend of Damasus, the bishop of the church of Rome, and continued with him till the bishop's death.

Then Jerome undertook the instruction in Christianity of a large class of distinguished ladies connected with the first families of Rome. Most of them were brought to a knowledge of the truth through his teaching, and became his warm and life-long friends. One of these, a wealthy widow lady named Paula, became especially interested in him. He had been the means of her conversion, and she used her money freely in helping him to carry on the good work in which he was engaged. When, in the year 386, Jerome concluded to go to the Holy Land and spend the rest of his life there, Paula and her daughter, and several of the other ladies who had been under his instruction in Rome, made up their minds to go with him. He went to Palestine, and chose Bethlehem as the place of his abode. There his friend Paula founded four convents for nuns, and one monastery, which she put under the charge of Jerome. He made his home there for the remainder of his days; and there he began, carried on, and finished the important work of translating and issuing the Latin, or, as it is called, the Vulgate version of the Bible. After this he remained there a happy, useful man till the year 420, when, at the age of eighty, he ceased from his labours and entered into " the rest that remaineth for the people of God."

Such are the leading facts in the history of Jerome.

In these facts we see illustrations of three interesting truths.

1. We see, in the experience of this good man, *how God guides his people by his providence.*

Jerome had a remarkable guidance in this way. In his early life, after he had joined the Church, he was very much given to the study of the writings of Cicero and other pagan authors. If he had continued to be absorbed in those studies, it would have been injurious to his Christian character, and would have interfered greatly with his usefulness. He had no earthly friend to give him wise counsel on this subject. But God, his heavenly Friend, did it for him. And he did it in this way: One night Jerome had a dream. In this dream he thought that he died and entered the heavenly world. An angel met him as he entered, and led him to the throne of God to be judged. He thought God told him that the chief fault he had to find with him was that he had studied the writings of Cicero and other pagan authors more than he had studied the Bible, and that the mistake he had made in doing this would interfere greatly with his happiness for ever. Then he awoke, and was greatly distressed at the thought of what he had been taught in that dream. He made a vow at once that he would turn over a new leaf—would give up the study of those pagan writers, and devote himself to the diligent and faithful study of the Scriptures. For years after this he never looked at one of those works of which he had before been so fond. If Jerome had not been led to make this change in his studies, he would not have been prepared for the great work he had to do of making a new translation of the Bible. This was the way in which God, by his providence, guided Jerome. And there are many ways in which the providence of God works for the guidance and protection and blessing of his people. Here is an illustration of this :—

On one occasion the good poet Cowper was unsettled in his mind. He felt so unhappy that he resolved to go to the river Thames and drown himself. He ordered a coachman, who was well acquainted with London, to drive him to Blackfriars' Bridge. Strangely enough, the man drove all over London but could not find the bridge. Then Cowper's mind changed, and he told the driver to take him home. When he reached his room he felt sure that God's providence had been working to save his life ; and then he sat down and wrote that beautiful hymn which begins thus :—

> " God moves in a mysterious way,
> His wonders to perform."

Here is another incident which shows us by what little things God's providence sometimes works. A missionary in Jamaica was walking one dark night along a dangerous road which had a steep precipice on one side of it several hundred feet deep. He could not see as he went on where he was treading. A single misstep might plunge him down the precipice, and so put an end to his work; but a little insect, called the candle-fly, came to his relief. It flew before him very near the ground, and the feeble light which it shed along his path was enough to show him where it was safe for him to tread. The little creature never left him till the danger was all past. Here we see how true it is that God can make *all things* work together for good to those who love him.

2. The second interesting truth we find illustrated in Jerome's history is *how God provides help for his servants in the work they have to do for him.*

We see this in what Jerome's friend Paula did for him. She belonged to one of the most distinguished families in Rome, being descended from the famous Scipios and Gracchi. She was very wealthy, and lived in one of the finest houses in that great city; but when she became a Christian she gave up the world with its vanities and pleasures, and devoted herself and her large means to doing good in various ways. She became the life-long friend of Jerome, because he was the instrument which God made use of to bring her to a knowledge of the Saviour. During the years in which Jerome lived in Rome, she insisted on his making her house his home, which he did. And we have seen how she provided for him in Bethlehem. The closing years of his life, spent there, were years of great usefulness; but the good which he did then would never have been accomplished if it had not been for the help afforded him by his friend Paula.

God's promise to each of his servants is, " I will help thee " (Isa. xli. 10).   He helps his people himself, by the grace and strength which he gives them ; and he helps them in many other ways.   The prophet Elijah had a singular experience of this.   On one occasion he had to live for months all alone in a desert place, because the king of Israel had deter-mined to kill him if he could find him.   There was water for Elijah to drink there, but there was no food for him to eat ; and so God helped this prophet by causing the ravens to bring him bread and meat, every morning and every evening, during all the many months he had to stay there.   Now the God who is able to work out his plans in such a way as this can never be at a loss to provide help for his servants in all their times of need.

3. The only other point we would refer to, as illus-trated in the life of Jerome, is *the importance of find-ing out what our life-work is to be, and then of faith-fully attending to it.*

This is what Jerome did.   The great work which he was raised up to accomplish, and with which his name is particularly associated, was the translating and issuing of the Latin version of the Bible, which is called the Vulgate.   The version of the Scriptures which had been used before his time was called " the

Septuagint." This is one of the oldest versions of the Bible in existence. It is said to have been prepared in the third century before Christ. The word Septuagint means " seventy." This name was given to it because seventy learned men are said to have been appointed by the authorities of the Jewish Church for the purpose of preparing this copy of the Old Testament Scriptures. It had for centuries been of great service to the Church in all countries where the Greek language was used; but in the time of Jerome the Latin tongue generally prevailed in western Europe. The Greek language was very little used in that part of the world. The people had only the Old Latin version, called the Itala, in which to read in their own language the wonderful works of God. A better version of the Bible, therefore, in the common language of the people, was very greatly needed. And when Jerome brought out his Vulgate, or Latin version of the Scriptures, in the language then generally used, he was conferring the greatest amount of good on uncounted myriads of people for many generations. That was his great life-work. He had attempted, from time to time, to prepare translations of different portions of God's Word; and the efforts which he thus made all helped to impress upon his mind the idea of the necessity which existed for a new translation of the, whole Bible. And so, when he found himself comfortably settled in his quiet home at Bethlehem, he determined to take up this work. He went patiently and perseveringly on with it, year after year, till the work was done, and the Latin edition of the Bible, the Vulgate, was given to the Church and the world as the great life-work of this good man.

God generally has something special for his people to do, which may be called their life-work. We see illustrations of this both in the Bible and out of it. When we look in the Bible we see that Noah's life-work was to build the ark. Joseph's was to make preparation for the wants of the people in Egypt, the surrounding nations, and his own kindred, during those years of famine. The life-work of Moses was to deliver the nation of Israel from the bondage of Egypt, and to give to them the divine law, and lead them through the wilderness to Canaan. So we might range through the Bible and point out the special life-work of each of God's servants whose history is there given.

And we find the same outside of the Bible. There was Martin Luther; his life-work was to bring about the great Protestant Reformation. Robert Raikes's life-work was to put the Sunday-school machinery in operation. John Williams's work was to introduce the gospel among group after group of beautiful islands in the South Pacific Ocean. Robert Moffat's was to do the same in Southern Africa. And if we become the faithful servants of the Lord Jesus Christ, and offer, each of us for himself or herself, the same prayer which the apostle Paul offered after his conversion, " Lord, what wilt thou have me to do ? " he who led Paul then and Jerome afterwards to find out what their life-work was to be, and to do it, will answer our prayer in the same way.

XVII.

Augustine of Numidia.

Born 354 (?); Died 430 (?).

AUGUSTINE is the last of the noble men of the
early Church in the East that we propose to
consider at present; but among all the famous heroes
of whom we have spoken, there was no one who possessed a nobler character or exercised a greater influence for good than Augustine.

A popular writer of our own day says of him:
"He was the most intellectual of all the fathers of
the early Church.   He was the great oracle of the
Latin Church, and has exercised a leading control
over the thoughts of the Christian world for a thousand years.   He is referred to with equal authority
by both Catholics and Protestants.   His penetrating
genius, his comprehensive views of truth, and his
marvellous power as a teacher of it, place him among
the immortal benefactors of mankind; while his
humanity, his charity, and his piety have endeared
him to the hearts of the Christian world."

Augustine was born in the town of Tagaste, in

Numidia, one of the northern provinces of Africa. The name of the town has since been changed, and it is now known as Bona, a fortified town surrounded by strong walls forty feet high and about two miles in circumference. His family were in moderate circumstances. His father was an idolater; but his mother, well known by her name as Monica, was one of the most earnest and devoted Christians that ever adorned and blessed the Church. His father determined to secure for him the best education that could be had; and after going through the first-class schools in his native town, he was sent to Carthage and then to Rome to finish his education. Augustine did not follow the instructions of his pious mother, but, led astray by erroneous teachers, fell into worldly, gay, and sinful habits of life, to the great grief of his affectionate and pious mother, and to his own serious injury. He never got back from these evil ways till he was over thirty years of age. While professor of rhetoric at Milan, he became a Platonist, studied the Bible, and then he became a Christian, and was baptized and ordained to the ministry, and was soon known as the most eloquent and successful preacher of that day. Not long after this he was chosen as the bishop of the church in Hippo, a town in the neighbourhood of his native place. He occupied that important position for the rest of his life.

These are the leading facts in the life of Augustine; and when we come to look more closely into them,

we find therein striking illustrations of a practical
and instructive character.

1. We see illustrated in Augustine's history *the importance of early piety*. There is no greater blessing
that any of us can have in this life than to be brought
to know and love the Saviour while we are young.
It is true, as Watts says in one of his beautiful
hymns, that

> " 'Twill save us from a thousand snares
>   To mind religion young ;
>   Grace will preserve our following years,
>   And make our virtues strong."

We could not have a better illustration of this than
we find in the case of Augustine. If he had only
followed his mother's teachings, and had sought to
know and love the Saviour while he was a boy at
home, the early years of his life, like those of his later
experience, would have been happy and useful years.
But instead of this, when he left home to go on with
his education, he was like a ship that goes to sea without chart or rudder, and the captain of which does
not know what port to sail for. In refusing to come
to Jesus in his youth, Augustine was turning his back
on the only true light ever given to us in regard to
God and the soul and eternity. Then he went wandering on along dark and dangerous paths. He was
led into sinful and sorrowful habits of life, which
became a burden of sorrow to him through all the
rest of his life, and almost broke his mother's heart.

What bitter tears she must have shed over her way-
ward, unhappy, sinful boy ! But she never ceased to
pray for him, and never gave up the hope that he
would be brought back from his erring ways at last.
Augustine disobeyed the command, " Remember now
thy Creator in the days of thy youth ; " and the
result was that he had to pass through years of sin
and sorrow before he became a Christian. And so it
will always be. The good Mr. Jay says, " Youth is
the spring-time of life ; and this must determine what
the glory of summer, the abundance of autumn, and
the provision for winter shall be. Youth is the seed-
time, and ' whatsoever a man soweth, that shall he
also reap.' Everything of importance in after life is
affected by early piety."

2. We see strikingly illustrated in the history of
Augustine *the blessed influence of a pious mother.*
Earnest, intelligent piety was the most prominent
feature in the character of Monica, the mother of
Augustine. Like Hannah, the mother of Samuel, she
consecrated her infant son to the Lord, and then
devoted herself to his religious education. She was
instrumental in the conversion of her husband a year
before his death ; and then her heart went out in
earnest and unceasing longings for the salvation of
her son. His youth, as we have said, was given up
to dissipation. He had embraced the errors of a sect
called Manicheans, which she feared would be the
ruin of his soul. For thirty years she was engaged

in unceasing prayers and efforts for his conversion. Her heart sank within her when it seemed at times as if her prayers were not to be answered. But at last, when her son was over thirty years of age, she heard that he had renounced his erroneous views, and had given up his sinful ways, and was earnestly seeking the Saviour. He was then at Milan, in Italy. Thither his mother hastened to him. He told her all about the long struggle through which he had passed, and the resolution he had now made to devote the rest of his life to the service of his God and Saviour. We can imagine something of the overflowing gladness of his mother's heart on finding that her life-long prayers had been answered at last. She was present at his baptism and at his ordination. Who can tell the joy that must have thrilled her bosom then? Not long after this, when Augustine was about to return to Africa, his native land, his mother was taken sick, and after a short illness passed away from earth, repeating, as she died, the words of good old Simeon, when he held the infant Saviour in his arms and said, " Lord, now lettest thou thy servant depart in peace ; for mine eyes have seen thy salvation."

No woman has ever been dearer to the Christian Church than Monica, the saintly mother of Augustine; and no mother ever conferred a greater blessing on the Church than she did in her untiring efforts and prayers for her son's conversion. We shall see this presently, when we come to speak of the wonderful amount of good which he did, not only in his own generation, but also in the generations that have followed him. Pious mothers have always been the greatest blessing to the Church. The extent to which their influence has reached none can tell. John and Charles Wesley, the famous founders of the Methodist Church, owed all their usefulness to the influence of their mother's piety. So it was with Philip Doddridge and John Newton, and so it has been all through the history of the Church and the world. We cannot thank God too much for pious mothers.

> " The mother, in her office, holds the key
> Of the soul ; and she it is who stamps the coin
> Of character, and makes the being who would be a savage
> But for her gentle care, a Christian man."

3. We see illustrated in the history of Augustine that *we never can begin our real life-work until we become true Christians.* Look at the course which Augustine pursued. He was going from one place to another, and engaging first in this employment and then in that ; but he had no definite end in view, till he found the Saviour and gave himself to him. Then he had a clear view of what his life-work was to be, and he gave himself up to it at once. This is generally the case. We see how plainly it was so in the experience of the apostle Paul. He had been sitting at the feet of Gamaliel to learn all about the Jewish

laws. He was one of the strictest of the sect of the Pharisees, and a faithful attendant on all the outward duties of religion. But this was not what he was sent into the world for. What this was he never found out till Jesus appeared to him on his way to Damascus. Then his eyes were opened and his heart was changed, and he offered the earnest prayer, " Lord, what wilt thou have me to do ? " In answer to this prayer it was revealed unto him that he was chosen of God his Saviour, " to bear his name before Gentiles and kings, and the children of Israel." The commission given by Christ to the twelve apostles was repeated to him. He was told to " go into all the world, and preach the gospel to every creature." *That* was his life-work ; but he never understood it till he bowed in penitence at the foot of the cross and gave himself to Jesus. Now what was true of the great apostle and of the saintly Augustine, is equally true of us all. We never can find out what our life-work is to be till we become true Christians. This is what Charles Wesley was realizing when he wrote these sweet lines :—

" Lord, in the strength of grace,
　With a glad heart and free,
Myself, my residue of days,
　I consecrate to thee.

" Thy ransomed servant, I
　Restore to thee thine own :
And from this moment live or die
　To serve my God alone."

Augustine never found out what his life-work was to be till he became a true Christian ; and it is just the same with us all.

4. We see illustrated in the life of Augustine that *when we begin in earnest to seek God, he is always ready in helping us to find him.* When Augustine left his mother's home and gave up the study of the Bible, he spent years in trying to find out the truth about God and the soul among the different schools of philosophy. But his efforts were all unavailing. He found no comfort or satisfaction anywhere. There was no ground on which he could rest. Nothing could give peace to his troubled conscience, or inspire him with hope for the future. This state of things continued till he left Rome and went to Milan to occupy a position which had been offered him as lecturer on rhetoric. Here he became acquainted with the famous Ambrose, who was bishop of the church there. After hearing him preach in public, and having conversations with him in private, for the first time in his life the light of truth began to shine feebly on his path. But with a troubled conscience and a mind oppressed with doubts and fears, he was in great distress and knew not what to do. In this troubled state he retired one day to a lonely spot in his garden. There he threw himself on the ground and earnestly asked God to help him. Then he seemed to hear a voice saying unto him, " Take and read, take and read." Having a copy of the New

Testament with him, he opened it at one of the epistles of St. Paul, and read these words : "Put ye on the Lord Jesus Christ, and make not provision for the flesh, to fulfil the lusts thereof" (Rom. xiii. 14). Then he bowed in penitence and faith before Christ, asking that his sins might be pardoned, his heart renewed, and that grace might be given him to be God's faithful servant. At once the light shone in upon his darkness ; his burden was removed, and peace and joy in believing filled his soul. And here we see how ready God was to help Augustine as soon as he began in earnest to seek him. And what God did for him in this respect, he is ready to do for all who are really trying to find him. His precious promise is, "Ye shall seek me, and find me, when ye shall search for me with all your heart" (Jer. xxix. 13). It is a blessed thing to find a truth like this so strikingly illustrated in the life of this noble hero of the early Church.

5. The only other point to which I would refer as illustrated in the history of Augustine is that *when we engage heartily in God's service, there is no telling how much good we may be able to do.* The turning-point in the life of Augustine began when he became a Christian and was baptized and joined the Church, in the thirty-fourth year of his age. Soon after this he went back to Africa, his native country. There, after he had been some time actively and successfully engaged in the duties of the ministry, he was chosen

bishop of the church in Hippo, a town not far from the place of his birth. This he held for thirty-five years, and with it his life of special usefulness began.

A popular writer of our own day speaks of Augustine thus:—" As a bishop he won universal admiration. Councils could do nothing without his presence. Emperors condescended to sue for his advice. He wrote letters to all parts of Christendom. He was alike saint, oracle, prelate, and preacher. He laboured day and night, living simply but without monkish austerity. At table, reading and literary conferences were preferred to secular conversation. His person was accessible. He interested himself in everybody's troubles, and visited the forlorn and miserable. He was indefatigable in reclaiming those who had gone astray. He won every heart by his kindness and charity, and captivated every mind by his eloquence ; so that Hippo, a little African town, was no longer 'least among the cities of Judah,' for her bishop was consulted from the very ends of the earth, and his influence went forth through the world to heal divisions and establish the faith of the wavering. He was indeed a father of the universal Church."

And then Augustine did great good by the noble way in which he opposed the prevailing errors of that age. The Manicheans, the Donatists, and the Pelagians were the principal sects then teaching erroneous doctrines. We have not time to enter into the details of their teaching. But Augustine pointed out their errors, and set forth the real truth of the Scriptures on the points at issue, in the clearest, strongest, and most successful way. And in the work thus accomplished, he was an untold blessing to the Church in those days.

And then by his writings he has been a blessing to the Church through all the many centuries that have passed away from his own time to the present. His letters, his work on the Psalms, on the Trinity, his "Confessions," and his "City of God," have been a fountain of unfailing blessing to the Church.

Moreover, he lived the doctrines which he preached and of which he wrote. He completely triumphed over the temptations which once overcame him. No one could ever remember an idle word from his lips after his conversion. He died in the year 430, in the seventy-sixth year of his age, full of visions of the unspeakable beauty of that blessed state to which for more than forty years his soul had been constantly soaring.

"Thus ceased to flow," said a writer of his own age, "that river of eloquence which had watered the thirsty fields of the Church; thus passed away the glory of preachers, the master of doctors, and the light of scholars; thus fell the courageous combatant, who with the sword of truth had given heresy a mortal blow; thus set this glorious sun of Christian doctrine, leaving the world in darkness and in tears."

XVIII.

Patrick, the Apostle of Ireland.

BORN 372 OR 373 (?); DIED 493 (?).

THERE are two other heroes of the early Church which may well be considered in our list, for they were used to give a knowledge of the gospel of Jesus to a portion of the people in the British Islands, by whom our own country was afterwards settled.

In the fifth century of the Christian era there flourished one of the most interesting characters in the history of the Church in Western Europe. He was called *Saint* Patrick, "the apostle of Ireland." A great many fancies and fables have been connected with his name. These we shall avoid as far as possible, and after glancing at the well-known facts of his history, shall speak very briefly of several things connected with him which had much to do with the great usefulness that marked his life.

This faithful servant of God is said to have been born on the 5th of April, in the year 373. He belonged to a very good family. His father and grandfather were both ministers of the gospel. The place of his birth is supposed to have been Kirkpatrick, near Dumbarton, in Scotland. A band of robbers prowling about that part of the country took him prisoner and carried him over to Ireland, when he was about fifteen years of age. There they sold him to an Irish farmer, who made him keeper of his flocks by day and by night. During those years of his early sojourn in Ireland he learned well the language of the country, and became greatly interested in its welfare; and thus the way was prepared for the great work which he was afterwards the instrument in accomplishing for the good of Ireland.

After six years of hard life in the service of the man to whom he had been sold, he managed to escape and return to his own land and to his father's house. Here, some two years after this, he formed the design of devoting his life to the work of converting Ireland to the religion of the gospel. Then we are told by some that he went over to the Continent, and pursued his studies under the care of his mother's uncle, St. Martin, the bishop of Tours, and that by him he was ordained to the ministry. By others it is said that he went to Rome and was commissioned by Pope Celestine to the work of evangelizing Ireland. It is hard to get at the exact truth in regard to some of these things; but we know certainly that he did go to Ireland and began his missionary work there about 432 A.D.

He preached and laboured there with such remarkable success that before his death the whole country was brought under the influence of the gospel. He baptized the kings or chiefs of Dublin and Munster and the seven sons of the chief of Connaught. His custom was always to strive to bring the chiefs of a particular district to a knowledge of the truth first, and then with their help to try to reach the people. The story about his driving the frogs and venomous reptiles from the island by the waving of his staff or crosier must be put down among the many fables that have been written concerning him. About his age at the time of his death different accounts have been given. Some of these represent him as dying when he was between seventy and eighty, while others state that he was over a hundred years old when he died. But all agree in stating that whatever the year was, the *day* of his death was the 17th of March. When this is spoken of as "St. Patrick's Day," it means not the day of his birth, but the day of his death. Such are the chief facts in the life of this famous man.

And now, let us look at some things connected with "the apostle of Ireland," which had much to do with making him so successful in the great work of his life.

1. The first of these was *his early piety.*

He began to serve God when he was quite young. He had learned to know and love the Saviour before he was stolen away from his father's home and sold as a servant or captive, in his fifteenth year ; and when that great trouble came upon him, he was ready for it. He knew what to do, and where to turn for help and comfort. If a vessel is driven suddenly out to sea, without a chart or a compass on board, then those who are in that vessel must have a trying time. They will not know which way to go, or how to steer their vessel. But how different their condition will be if they only have a chart and compass with them! The chart will show them which way to go, and the compass will help them to steer their vessel in that way. But when we learn to know and love Jesus, he will be our chart and compass in the voyage of life before us. His presence and blessing are the things most essential to our success. It is true, as the hymn says, that

> " 'Twill save us from a thousand snares,
>   To mind religion young;
> Grace will preserve our following years,
>   And make our virtues strong."

Patrick, " the apostle of Ireland," had the great blessing of early piety, and this had much to do with the remarkable success which attended his work.

2. The second thing which led to this success was *the spirit of prayer which he exercised.*

When he was a youthful captive in Ireland, he speaks of himself thus: " I was employed every day in tending sheep; I used to stay in the woods and on the mountain. I prayed frequently. The love and fear of God and faith in him increased so much, and

the spirit of prayer grew so strong in me, that I often
prayed more than twenty times in the day, and almost
as often in the night.   I frequently rose to prayer in
the woods before daylight, in rain and frost and snow.
I feared no evil, nor was there any sloth in me.   I
felt that God was with me."

We have another illustration of how he was helped
by prayer in the account he gives of the way in
which he escaped from his captivity in Ireland.   " I
made up my mind," he says, " to leave the man with
whom I had lived for six years.   I went in the power
of the Lord to look for the vessel that would take me
away.   I found the vessel, and asked for a passage.
The captain was angry, and said I could not go.   As
I turned away, my heart was lifted up in prayer to
God.   I had not gone far when one of the sailors
came after me.   He called to me and said, ' Come
back, for we want you to go with us.'   I went, and
was kindly received ; and so the way was opened for
me to return to my home in Scotland."

And when we think of this good man as going on
with his work in Ireland, in the exercise of such a
spirit of prayer as this, we need not wonder at his
success.   Eliot, the missionary to the Indians, said,
" Prayer and pains can do anything."   It is true, as
one has said, " Prayer has divided seas, rolled up flow-
ing rivers, made flinty rocks gush into fountains,
quenched flames of fires, muzzled the mouths of lions,
stopped the moon and the sun in their courses, burst

open iron gates, and brought legions of angels down
from heaven. Prayer brought one man from the
bottom of the sea, and carried another in a chariot of
fire to heaven. What is there that prayer cannot
do ? " It is true, as the hymn says, that

> " Prayer makes the darkened cloud withdraw,
> Prayer climbs the ladder Jacob saw,
> Gives exercise to faith and love,
> Brings every blessing from above."

And when we think of Patrick as going on with his
work under the influence of such a spirit of prayer as
he exercised, we need not wonder at the success which
crowned his labours.

3. The only other thing of which we have now
room to speak, as leading to the success which attended his labours, was *the use he made of the Word
of God.*

In the few writings of his that remain we find
nothing that agrees with the teaching of the Romish
Church. There is no mention made of the pope of
Rome. Not a word is said about the doctrine of pur-
gatory, or confession to the priests, as necessary to
salvation. Nothing about what Romanists call tran-
substantiation, or the belief that in the sacrament of
the Lord's Supper the bread and wine are changed
into the actual body and blood of Christ, and nothing
about the worship of the Virgin Mary, can be found in
his books. Instead of making any reference to these
Romish errors, his writings abound in the simplest

statements of gospel truth.   The Scriptures are treated
by him with the profoundest reverence.   He speaks
of them as intended by God for the free use of *all his
people*.   In support of his teachings he never appealed
to any other authority than that of the written word.
No matter what popes or councils or the fathers said,
the simple declaration of Scripture, " *Thus saith the
Lord*," was sufficient for him.   This settled everything.   In the few chapters of his Confession alone,
there are no less than thirty-five quotations from the
Holy Scriptures.   And it was because he made such
a free use of " the sword of the Spirit " that he was so
successful in his contest with the erroneous opinions
and practices of heathenism.

To illustrate this part of our subject, and show
how clear the views of Patrick were of " the truth as
it is in Jesus," I will quote here a few lines from a
hymn said to have been written by him :—

> " Christ with me, Christ before me,
>   Christ behind me, Christ within me,
>   Christ beneath me, Christ above me,
>   Christ at my right, Christ at my left.
>   Christ in the heart of every man
>   Who thinks of me ;
>   Christ in the mouth of every man
>   Who speaks to me ;
>   Christ in every eye that sees me,
>   Christ in every ear that hears me."

And a man who was so full of Christ, and had so
much to say of him, could not fail of being successful
in bringing others to him.

And when we think of the early piety of this faithful servant of God, of the spirit of prayer which he exercised, and of the use he made of the Word of God, we see three elements of the success which attended his missionary labours in Ireland.

XIX.

Columba, the Apostle of Scotland.

BORN A.D. 521 (?); DIED 597 (?).

IN the sixth century after Christ, God raised up another famous Christian hero in the British Islands. The most interesting and prominent character belonging to this period of the Church's history is Columba, or, as he is generally called, Saint Columba. This title was given him, not after his death, as is often done in the Romish Church, but during his lifetime, for the eminent piety which marked his character.

It is remarkable that Patrick, whose character we considered in the previous chapter, was born in Scotland, yet devoted his life to the work of Christianizing Ireland; while Columba was born in Ireland, but spent his days in the work of Christianizing Scotland.

We may consider very briefly the leading facts in the life of this good man, and then notice some of the lessons we may gather from it.

Columba was born in Donegal, in Ireland, in the year 521. He was connected with a princely or royal family in that part of Ireland. His mother was connected with a princely family in Argyleshire, Scotland; and it was no doubt the thought of his mother's connection with that country which gave rise to his interest in it, and led him to devote his life to its welfare. When he was quite young, Columba was put under the care of a faithful minister of the gospel to receive his education. Then he was led to know and love the Saviour, and to give his heart and life to him. He entered the ministry as soon as he was of age, and the first years of his ministerial life were occupied in the work of preaching the gospel in Ireland. He went through the districts of Leinster, Connaught, Meath, and other parts, making known the truth as it is in Jesus, and calling on the people to repent and believe in Christ. He was very successful in this work. Like Patrick, his custom was, when he formed a church in any neighbourhood, to have a school established in connection with it. And before he went to Scotland he had been the means of organizing one hundred churches and schools in different parts of Ireland, which were so many fountains of blessing to the neighbourhoods in which they were established.

In the year 563, when he was more than forty years of age, Columba, with a company of twelve friends, chosen to help him in his work, left Ireland

and went over to Scotland to begin his great life-work there. He made his head-quarters on the celebrated island of Iona. This belongs to the well-known group of the Hebrides, off the western shore of Scotland. Iona is a little island, only about three miles long and a mile and a half broad. It was given to Columba by the king who reigned over the Picts in the northern part of Scotland. It has now a population of about five hundred people. Here Columba founded a church and built what was called a monastery. This was a sort of school or college, which became one of the most famous seats of learning in all that part of Europe. It was kept up for several hundred years after his death with great success, and was the means of doing a wonderful amount of good. The earnest piety and the useful learning which were spread by these institutions, and the many ruins of churches and schools once existing here, have made this island of Iona a sort of classic ground, a place of great interest to travellers, who love to visit it. From Iona as his head-quarters, Columba spent the rest of his busy life in making missionary journeys through the surrounding islands and other parts of Scotland. He preached the gospel, and was the means of establishing churches and opening schools wherever he went. He kept up these labours perseveringly till his death, which took place in the seventy-eighth year of his age.

Such were the leading facts in the life of this good

man. We may set him before us as an example worthy of our imitation in three important respects.

1. We find in Columba *an example of untiring industry.*

This marked his whole course. He began, continued, and ended his life in the exercise of this spirit. In all his plans of usefulness, and in his carrying on of his missionary labours, this industry was ever to be seen. Whatever he began to do, he persevered in doing till it was accomplished. When at home, between his missionary journeys, he employed himself diligently in study. The art of printing was not then known, and the pen had to take the place of the press in multiplying such books as were needed. Columba used his pen so industriously, that in the course of his busy life he had with his own hand written out no less than three hundred volumes. And so earnest was he in trying to further the interests of religion and learning in this way, that he continued to employ himself thus to the end of his life. Only a few days before his death he was busily engaged in writing out a copy of the Psalms of David to be used in one of his schools. And this love of knowledge he tried to get others about him to cherish also. His seminary at Iona was a fountain from which streams of learning and religion flowed forth on every hand. Students came to Iona from all parts of Scotland and England, and even from the continent of Europe; and when their studies were finished, they went forth to spread abroad on the right hand and on the left the blessings of knowledge and religion which they had received there.

And Columba taught to all about him the same industry which he practised himself. Hence, with this untiring industry in himself and in those about him, we need not wonder that he was successful in all that he did. On the walls of the celebrated temple of Delphos in Greece there used to be inscribed this motto : " Nothing is impossible to industry."

2. We have in Columba *an example of unfailing kindness.* This idea is wrapped up in his very name. Columba is the Latin name for a dove ; and the dove has always been considered as the type or emblem of kindness or gentleness. Hence we read that when our Saviour was baptized in the river Jordan, the heavens were opened above him and the Holy Ghost descended in a bodily shape like a dove and abode upon him. " The gentleness of Christ" was a chief element of his character ; and it will be so with all who are his true servants. It was so with Columba. The name first given him as a child had only two syllables in it. He was called Colum. But as he was growing up, he showed so much kindness and gentleness that his parents concluded to add another syllable to his name, and called him Columba, " the dove." And he well deserved this name. The spirit that dwelt in him was a gentle and loving spirit.

This gave a sweet expression to his countenance, and made his voice and manner always pleasing.

His disciples and servants he always spoke of as his " children " or " brethren." Everything connected with them became an object of interest to him. If he knew that they were in trouble or danger, he would engage in earnest prayer for them. When they were labouring in the field, he would go out and cheer and encourage them in their work. He always had a kind word for every one. He was often called upon to settle disputes which were likely to end in trouble and bloodshed. And he was always successful in these efforts.

A short time before his death a little incident occurred which strikingly illustrates the effect of his kindness. When going home from church one day he was so feeble that he was obliged to stop and rest by the way. As he was sitting under the shadow of a tree, an old horse that had long been accustomed to carry milk to the monastery, and had experienced Columba's kindness, came up to him and laid its head upon his breast as if he wanted to say, " Good-bye, old master ; I'm sorry you are going to leave us." His servant was going to drive the animal away ; but Columba said, " No ; let him alone. He only wants to show that he is sorry to lose me." And then he patted it gently on the head, and said, " Good-bye." How true it is, as the good Henry Martyn said, that " the power of gentleness is irresistible ! "

> " Speak gently—it is better far
>   To rule by love than fear ;
>   Speak gently—let no harsh words mar
>   The good we might do here."

3. Columba comes before us also as *an example of earnest piety.*

We see this in the early part of his Christian life. We have spoken of him as belonging to the royal family of the tribe among whom he was born. As the eldest son in that family, he was the heir of the crown. He had become a Christian before his father died ; but in the state of feeling then existing among his people, they were unwilling to have a Christian for their king. He found that either Christ or the crown must be given up. And like the apostle Paul, he " conferred not with flesh and blood." He clung to Christ and let the crown go. Here he showed his earnest piety. This was the foundation on which the character of this good man was built ; and there is no better foundation on which a good character can be built.

The piety of Columba was not confined to Sabbath or the sanctuary. He sought to sanctify everything by the Word of God and prayer. If he mounted his cart for a journey, he first asked God's blessing on his journey. When he entered the barn and saw the heaps of grain there, he lifted up his heart to God and thanked him for it. He began no work and engaged in no business without asking God's blessing upon it. If he administered medicine to the sick, it was always accompanied with a prayer to God who healeth. His preaching was always preceded and followed by prayer.

And when we think of Columba's untiring industry, his unfailing kindness, and his earnest piety, we need not wonder at the success which crowned his labours.

THE END.

Other Solid Ground Titles

In addition to the book in your hand, Solid Ground is honored to offer other uncovered treasure, many for the first time in more than a century:

ANNALS OF THE AMERICAN BAPTIST PULPIT *by William B. Sprague*
JESUS OF NAZARETH *by John A.. Broadus*
THE CHILD AT HOME by John S.C. Abbott
THE KING'S HIGHWAY: *The 10 Commandments for the Young* by Richard Newton
THE LIFE OF JESUS CHRIST FOR THE YOUNG by Richard Newton
LET THE CANNON BLAZE AWAY by Joseph P. Thompson
THE STILL HOUR: *Communion with God in Prayer* by Austin Phelps
COLLECTED WORKS of James Henley Thornwell (4 vols.)
CALVINISM IN HISTORY *by Nathaniel S. McFetridge*
OPENING SCRIPTURE: *Hermeneutical Manual by Patrick Fairbairn*
THE ASSURANCE OF FAITH *by Louis Berkhof*
THE PASTOR IN THE SICK ROOM *by John D. Wells*
THE BUNYAN OF BROOKLYN: *Life & Sermons of I.S. Spencer*
THE NATIONAL PREACHER: *Sermons from 2nd Great Awakening*
FIRST THINGS: *First Lessons God Taught Mankind Gardiner Spring*
BIBLICAL & THEOLOGICAL STUDIES *by 1912 Faculty of Princeton*
THE POWER OF GOD UNTO SALVATION *by B.B. Warfield*
THE LORD OF GLORY *by B.B. Warfield*
A GENTLEMAN & A SCHOLAR: *Memoir of J.P. Boyce* *by J. Broadus*
SERMONS TO THE NATURAL MAN *by W.G.T. Shedd*
SERMONS TO THE SPIRITUAL MAN *by W.G.T. Shedd*
HOMILETICS AND PASTORAL THEOLOGY *by W.G.T. Shedd*
A PASTOR'S SKETCHES 1 & 2 *by Ichabod S. Spencer*
THE PREACHER AND HIS MODELS *by James Stalker*
IMAGO CHRISTI *by James Stalker*
A HISTORY OF PREACHING *by Edwin C. Dargan*
LECTURES ON THE HISTORY OF PREACHING *by J. A. Broadus*
THE SCOTTISH PULPIT *by William Taylor*
THE SHORTER CATECHISM ILLUSTRATED *by John Whitecross*
THE CHURCH MEMBER'S GUIDE *by John Angell James*
THE SUNDAY SCHOOL TEACHER'S GUIDE *by John A. James*
CHRIST IN SONG: *Hymns of Immanuel from All Ages by Philip Schaff*
COME YE APART: *Daily Words from the Four Gospels by J.R. Miller*
DEVOTIONAL LIFE OF THE S.S. TEACHER *by J.R. Miller*

Call us Toll Free at 1-877-666-9469
Send us an e-mail at sgcb@charter.net
Visit us on line at solid-ground-books.com